Also by AC Benus

The Secret Melville Series
Seven filmscripts based on the sea novels of Herman Melville
ebook: ISBN 9781953389022; paperback: ISBN 9781953389039

Mojo
A modern reimagining of Petronius' ancient novel Satyricon *set in Trump's America of conmen, the conned, the ultra-rich, the sexy and the downright silly. "A laugh riot!"*
ebook: ISBN 9781734561074; paperback: ISBN 9781734561050

One Hundred and Fifty-Five Sonnets for Tony
A bold testament to love
ebook: ISBN 9781953389114; paperback: ISBN 9781953389107; hardback: ISBN 9781953389121

Demon Dream
Redemption and shared humanity shine in this retelling of a medieval Japanese legend
ebook: ISBN 9781953389138; paperback: ISBN 9781953389145

Mikhail Kraminsky, and other poems
Two collections of early poems exploring the pain of youth and being closeted
ebook: ISBN 9781953389152; paperback: ISBN 9781953389169

First Love: Poems for Ross
For everyone's first love; both bitter and sweet
ebook: ISBN 9781734561081; paperback: ISBN 9781734561098

Also by AC Benus

Hymenaios, or The Marriage of the God of Marriage
A Classical style myth in 2,600 lines of Blank Verse
ebook: ISBN 9781953389091; paperback: ISBN 9781953389084

Summer 2020 – Hell in a Handbasket
A contender for the Pulitzer Prize in poetry, 2021, this collection grapples with the year of pandemic, racial justice and environmental crisis
ebook: ISBN 9781953389015; paperback: ISBN 9781953389008

The Thousandth Regiment
A Translation of and Commentary on Hans Ehrenbaum-Degele's First World War Poems "Das tausendste Regiment"
ebook: ISBN 1657220583; paperback: ISBN 9781657220584

A Man in a Room and other poems
Verse following the year when the poet was 21 years old
ebook: ISBN 97817345103; paperback: ISBN 978173456107

The Easiest Thing in the World, and other poems
Marking the third anniversary of the Pulse Nightclub terror attack
ebook: ISBN 9781734561029; paperback: ISBN 9781734561036

Rima Fragmenta, or Fragments of a Rift
Fifty Sonnet for Kevin
ebook: ISBN 9781734561005; paperback: ISBN 9781734561012

Walks *With* Leporello

THOUGHTS ON LOVE, GOD & DOG

AN AIREDALE REMEMBERED
✑ AC Benus

an AC Benus Impression
San Francisco

*Grateful acknowledgement is here offered
for the support and encouragement
I've received on the literary site
www.gayauthors.org.*

ISBN 978-1-953389-26-8 (ebook)
ISBN 978-1-953389-25-1 (paperback)
ISBN 978-1-953389-27-5 (hardback)

Cover photo:
Unsplash.com – Xuan Nguyen

Back cover portrait of Leporello:
Copyright Amanda Jones Photography. All rights reserved.

Library of Congress Control Number: 2022911923

Walks With Leporello

From: AC Benus
Sent: Monday, May 9, 2011 4:40 PM
To: [...]
Subject: For all Leppy lovers . . .

It is with heavy heart and sluggish hand that I inform you of our loss. Leppy shook off his mortal coil Saturday evening. He died at home peacefully, surrounded by his family, knowing he was / is loved.

He lived to be 15 years, 6 months and 1 day old.

He is survived by Sunny and me and his two brothers, Figaro, age 3, and Masetto, age 9 months.

Our loss is heaven's gain, for after all, we were only permitted the chance to 'borrow' him for a while anyway.

We were / are lucky to have been / be so blessed.

AC and Sunny

ESSAY 1:
Eyes of an Airedale Person

I suppose I should start Tristram-Shandy-style, before the beginning. [1] But what exists before we are born? Life does. We drop in as characters in the fashion of Japanese novels, without intro-ductions or prefaces, and without any particular grand, let's tie this whole thing up, finales. We drop in on our own stories already in progress, and in which we only – at least at first – play a small part. We start as novices in our own tales, and if we are lucky, gain sight of ourselves through the eyes of others. As a newbie we may witness great acts of love and heartbreak, and interpret these wrongly as petty, self-serving ones – the question is always – how do we relate? The yardstick of our own experience measures our ability to love and see love in others, and this stick is mighty short in the beginning, but grows as we do. God with his universal divider placed firmly in his weary hand is the longest-lived, and consequently, the longest sufferer of heartbreak.

Max mouthed a tennis ball and nuzzled my crotch with it – gently – his huge brown eyes assessing my face frankly as I sat on his sofa. He glanced fleetingly at the parakeet to my right side, then back to me. Max was the father, or, to use the correct term, the *sire,* of the Airedale puppy we were there to meet and potentially adopt. Max, whose full name I was to later learn from his pedi-gree papers was *Max What-a-Dog Keisel,* stood in front of me a seeming Genesis-sized giant – well over 120 pounds and pro-portioned like a small calf might be. His ears were perfect folded handkerchiefs; silky coin purse on the outside and a flush healthy pink on the inside. Now with the ball in his mouth, his mouth in my crotch, the ears rode the back of his head in the classic expression of formal appraisal. He was interviewing me. Doing so to assure himself I was worthy of his issue – and by the way, what type of person was I?

The parakeet was his buddy, and later I saw Max, in a moment of boredom, go over to the cage and prop his nose against the bars. The cage occupant acted with a hell-to-pay ire for the invasion of his space, but it was all a friendly sham, a ritual of play, for in a few moments the parakeet was on the floor of his cage and using his beak to caress the big black nose of his big Airedale lug. Max closed his eyes momentarily, enjoying the tickling scratch, and the passing of love from the bird. Then it was over. With no fuss, Max stiffened, huffed through the bars and moved away. The bird flitted up to his perch and eyed Max's retreat.

Now here I was, pooped after a Saturday of relentless driving from San Francisco to Sebastopol, and then through backroads-tundra to this sofa and Sacramento. We, Sunny and I, had set up two appointments to look at puppies. We almost turned back a couple of hours out of Sebastopol because there we had met a sweet little girl we thought fit our bill. Here at 7:30 PM, for our 4:00 PM appointment, we knew instantly that Max's offspring was to be our companion dog. A second 'almost didn't happen' occurred as we rang the doorbell. The door opened and we were greeted with "We have to be someplace by 8, and were just leaving – we thought you weren't showing up." We were ushered in and greeted by Max, then by GB's Abby Gail Keisel, the pup's mom – or *dam* – and sat down. Abby was much more reserved and eyed us maternally, leaning against the sofa in calm participation.

I tried to take the ball. Wrong. Max would not release it. I tried again, and this time he shook his head violently like he was breaking the neck of a rag doll. So, I frowned and figured "Let him keep it then." What he did next startled me. He dropped the ball right into my hand. Why? I had given up, pooped out on his game. Consequently he made the rules easier so I could play too. I tossed the ball. He brought it back to me, and the whole scene of my trying to take the ball was repeated.

☙ ☙ ☙ ☙

It seemed to me there was never a time I didn't know about Airedales, but I suppose my first and very memorable introduction to their abilities came in high school, reading James Thurber's *The Dog That Bit People*. Muggs, their family Airedale circa 1917, was a tough cookie who patrolled the mean streets of

Columbus, Ohio, like a kingpin holding turf and prepared to fight and lick any challenger. The Thurber family's dog had the remarkable ability to regret. His mother, the one person Muggs never bit, always knew by his expression that he was sorry after having sunk his teeth into neighbors, salesmen, delivery men, cops and senators (yes, Muggs bit one of Ohio's U. S. Senators while he was campaigning in the Thurber home). [2]

My re-introduction to the subject came in January 1990. *Connoisseur Magazine* ran an article by Chip Brown praising the Airedale as a combination of "Style, Brains and Clownish Wit." [3] The piece's title apparently did not have room for Brave and Persevering, but Brown tells of Moujik, a Central American Airedale who, in the 1950s, caught a burglar by the wrist in the middle of the night, and detained him on the staircase until morning. Moujik had, the criminal later related, snuck up noise-lessly as the man took his first step on the stairs. He felt a dull ping, looked down and found a menacing Airedale attached to him. The dog growled under his breath with every twitch of struggle the man exhibited, and by morning, when the family found him, the would-be thief was a nervous wreck. Moujik, matters well in hand – or rather, well in mouth – hadn't felt it necessary to raise the alarm and deprive the household of its peaceful slumbers. Brown's subtitle states 'Everything One looks for in a Spouse,' and after we moved to San Francisco in 1995, Sunny suggested it was time for a puppy – "an Airedale?" I asked. "Of course," he said – 'Quiet dignity' Brown's article quoted, and 'The ebullient joy of life' – what else, but an Airedale?

౭   ౭   ౭   ౭

We met this Sacramento puppy. We saw the clear fact that he was the pick of the litter, strong, gentle and wide-eyed, and we were lucky a third time. This pup, as the prize among his littermates, left his parents and siblings' side first. However, the couple who took him home at six weeks began to have issues with their relationship and returned him at eight weeks. Here at the end of January 1996, Sunny and I sat with a breeder who used to live around the corner from us in San Francisco, and who, like us, had always raised dogs in a family of two daddies.

Yes, he was our puppy. Thrice moved, fate tricked away the obstacles to ensure he was going to live with us, no matter what.

We struck the bargain, exchanged a deposit check, shook hands, and Sunny and I prepared our household for baby's arrival. We would pick him up the following Saturday, January 27th, so Sunny made a bed with a slipcover decorated in the puppy's new name, and we bought food and bowls, a collar, leash, any and every thing a pup would need for his daily existence. I also picked out a humble stuffed canvas toy mouse. It had a rope tail and floppy ears with blue fabric on the inside, These were his first possessions. What a paradoxically long week I had to endure as it flew by in a blink: the last static charge of a life soon to be entirely different.

The day of pickup, we were early, having fetched the rental car at the crack of 6 AM when the place opened. At the sound of the doorbell, we received the same warm greeting from Max and Abby as the week before, and the same wide-eyed gambol from the puppy, who was exactly twelve weeks old that Saturday morning. Bruce Waggoner, the breeder, looking a bit misty-eyed, told us how the little family of dogs had played all morning. He had even gotten out his camcorder to capture the family romps. For we had seen this type of family play the week before. For insistence, one time the puppy had gone and climbed up on the bean bag chair, the leather one against which Abby Gail was already lying. A moment later, Max sidled over, pretending he saw no one around, and plopped down on the bag, causing a puppy-bounce and instant play amongst the three of them. Witnessing this, and the puppy's confidence, I knew instinctively that his long-term exposure to his parents and siblings was one of the ingredients allowing a well-adjusted dog to grow from puppyhood.

But, as we sat at the dining table, filling out the paperwork for the official transfer, I became distracted. It was hard to hear the information about the banana-flavored de-wormer we were to give the puppy, because Max was causing a fracas. He was pacing around, and each time the puppy came near him, he'd snap out a warning bark, and then turn his back on him. In a minute or two, Abby joined in. It seemed to me they were ganging up on the puppy and battering him. I thought to myself, based on what I had been reading in the puppy books, that we'd arrived at the right moment. Max, as the intact male – so the print experts warned – had to eventually see other males as his rivals and dominate them. And here Sunny and I were, right on time to 'rescue' the puppy from a dangerous situation. Bruce apologized, not knowing why they acted like this when their morning had been filled with such lovey-dovey play.

And so, we bundled our puppy up in the towel we had brought for him, and left Sacramento self-satisfied that we had done good for all involved.

I mentioned that the pick of the litter was back early, and from there all his nine siblings had been adopted one by one. He was held back because "the couple," a young man and woman, said they needed time to work out their interpersonal issues, but would return for him in a week or two. They never did, presumably splitting up, so our pup was the last to leave the side of Max and Abby Gail.

I said perspective is important, and my self-righteous reckoning of 'rescue' was seen through the novice eyes of a non-Airedale person. For years, many years, I wondered at Max's behavior, until at last, the experienced Airedale person I had evolved into, allowed me to see through *his* eyes. Max loved his children, he had been through loss – puppy after puppy, over and over again, and his hostile attitude to his young son when he saw Sunny and me reappearing at his house, was to prepare the puppy for being separated from his parents. Max grieved for his own impending loss by making his child ready to leave them. Acts of love, sometimes forced by others and out of our control, lead us to that beautiful perspective through others' eyes – a Godly perspective, with or without a ball in the mouth, with or without a nose in the crotch. As I write this, I imagine Max in his living room after we left him all those years ago. I see him wandering; avoiding the puppy's places; seeing him everywhere, yet knowing there is nowhere he can be seen. I imagine Max going over to the parakeet cage. The bird scratching his nose, and Max closing his eyes with the numbed pleasure afforded by routine. Family does continue; others do need us; and although it's cold comfort, it's comfort nonetheless.

ご ご ご ご

Of all my personal Airedale stories, fought for and won through dogged determination, or of all the many faithful Airedale accounts I have heard – like the bravery of Moujik – the example of Max's heartbreak turned to selfless act, to thoughts of his innocent child's emotional well-being before his own sadness, makes Max's story the greatest I know. Fifteen and a half years later, at the end of his pup's life, I relate to his grief best; to his loss. Now you have him again. Now I have a more proper perspective on the both of you. What I have gained through experience because of you is a much-lengthened yardstick with which to measure a proper deference for what I see. Thank you Max, what a dog, Keisel. Thank you. [4]

ESSAY II:
Fire Hydrants and Bougainvillea

The first rush of colors and sound; new people and sensations; new whirls of experience; all of this for our puppy, Leporello, was literal; all *new,* while for his human companions, it was a chance to see the mundane through his eyes with unsullied sight. But sadly, so too is the first exposure to fright and lonesomeness – to separation and doubt. There are scary things in the world. For us, the "what ifs" loomed large: what if he's lost; what if he runs into traffic; what if he encounters a bully dog who starts a fight and hurts him. But for Leppy, his frights were obstacles of menacing strangeness that darkly shadowed his path. What is a fire hydrant? Does it move; does it know I know? In time these frights work themselves out. Our human frights – our reactions to separation, to doubt and loneliness – these take more work; more time to resolve.

Considering the hundred or so pounds he would grow into, the little ten-pound puppy, on his towel, in my lap, seemed miniscule and fragile. Sunny drove most of the way back from Sacramento, Saturday, January 27th, 1996, while I sat with the new one. He mostly napped, but rose to his hind legs sometimes to put his front paws on the curve of the door where it became glass. He peered out on the rolling scenery, darkened by less than fair skies, with his ears alert and turned full-front. After a few moments, he'd glance at me, blink with lowered ears, then settle down again into a comfy ball on his towel. I expected signs of anxiety – panting, fidgeting and so on – but he was calm. Besides the periodic looking out the window, and the some-times-turned Bambi-eyes that went up to me with a questioning gaze, he was fine for the long drive. I'd stroke his silky head, and tell him we would soon be "Home."

I had the decidedly humdrum task of retracing the car's path through the city streets downtown, dropping it off, and taking the streetcar back home. These seemed mammoth under-

takings, because after depositing Sunny and pup at our front
door, there was nothing in the world I so wanted not to do than
leave them. But soon we were bundled against the gloomy
January evening and off for our first family walk. Because of his
age, and not having had his final Parvovirus inoculation, we
were to avoid any contact with other dogs; but walk we must.

☙ ☙ ☙ ☙

There is a magic street in San Francisco with a mere five
short blocks that points the way every urban landscape could
look, if the will were there to make it happen. This start of Noe
Street had its utility lines buried in the late 1970s under pressure from one of the first neighborhood associations in the
country. At the same time, they had the sidewalks widened into
mini plazas near the corners. But what makes the entire magic
are the towering and gracile ash trees planted at that time. Now
mature, they arch upwards from the Victorian facades to form a
three-story *allée* that everyone sighs just to be under. Every
street could be as polished as these few blocks are; it only takes
some people who care enough to do it.

So the puppy arrived at 128 Noe. It was his birthright to
mature under the ash boughs and be surrounded by the green
grass of several nearby parks. Later, after a couple of moves, I
could always tell he longed to return to our first home. For many
years after leaving this street, he'd turn into every travertine
stoop that resembled our Noe Street steps. None of them were
the correct one he hoped for, but such is life.

Even though, on this first evening with us, the pup had
not received any leash training, he trod along like a pro. We
began to practice the "sit at the curb" command (one he only
ever partially acquiesced to), and within a block, we encountered the first bogeyman of his later bad dreams. Yes, there at
the corner across from Duboce Park was the dingy-white trunk
of a threat. The moment Leppy spied the fire hydrant, he stopped, his ears went flat and tail went tucked; a whimper and a
faltering step backwards halted all progress. We cajoled, we
gently tugged, but the dog-to-be was frightened. Finally, after
much encouragement, he stiffened four limbs, straightened his
jelly spine and leaned nose-forward, sniffing and stretching inch
by inch as close as his firmly rooted back legs would allow. The
cold pylon did not flinch as little by little a waving of the head

allowed the inspector nose to do its job. Partially assured by the findings, the head recoiled and led the way for quickly scampering legs to scurry to the other side of the menace and pause in shaky reassessment. His eyes looked to us. "What was that? I don't think it likes us . . . . "

Beyond the hydrant though was the world of the park. The park that would be the most wonderful place for our dog in the whole world. His first sight was slightly from afar, as he couldn't meet any other dogs, but he witnessed myriad canines running after frisbees, balls and each other, all in a high and friendly frolic. Again he looked at us. "What is this place? Who are all those dogs and people?" His wide-eyed wonder imbued the scene for us with new curiosity. Who were all these people; how did they all raise such happy dogs?

There would be many more visits to Duboce Park and others – countless park visits – but only one first sight; only one time where the whole spectacle and promise was new.

🐾 🐾 🐾 🐾

I probably have avoided mentioning that Leppy was our first dog, the first dog I had in my life that was not the neighbors' or friends' but the first I had as mine in my twenty-seven years. Sunny had a terrier and a Cocker Spaniel when a small boy, but despite all my childhood requests, and despite the fact that my mom had had dogs for all the years before I was born, I grew up with only neighbor canines in my life. This goes to explain that books provided any (inadequate) grounding for my puppy expectations. One subject they all agreed upon was that the newly arrived puppy would suffer terribly from separation anxiety. The first night, according to the authorities, would be full of whining, yelping and general misery for the small one looking for mom, dad and siblings. So I was prepared to have a restless night.

After the park came dinnertime, and then – mind you, it's about 7:30 in the evening – the puppy laid his weary head down on Sunny's hand-made slipcovered pillow, and slept. With his back curled and his face tucked over his one and only toy, the canvas mouse, he was zonked out cold. We thought, "Okay, it's just a nap," but he stayed that way, despite gentle attempts at rousing. We just wanted to let him know that around eleven o'clock we were going to bed and to show him where we would be. The lights went out, and it was a long time before I relaxed. I kept listening for the first bark, yelp, or worse. I finally drifted off with the puppy, who slept at the foot of our bed, not having stirred an inch since after dinner.

Exhausted from forcing myself to doze lightly, I was deep in sleep at 3:00 AM when I roused to faint whimpering and toenails on the hardwood floor. I extended my arm from beneath the covers, held it out straight and gently called "Puppy." Soon I felt a moist little nose bump into my fingertips, then heard a settling down on the floor by my hand as rest again overcame Leporello. That was it. Never again did he show even the slightest separation anxiety. I suppose he dreamt of car-riding, of green grass and a looming metal shadow that night, but he was resting for the big day ahead of him – ahead for all of us.

ꝰ ꝰ ꝰ ꝰ

The worst of his dreams would occur sometime later, when he was about three years old. One night we awoke to the clear sounds of nightmare – voiceless barking in his sleep, floor thumping from his only partially turned-off running limbs, and twitching muzzle and nose. I got up and switched on the light. I didn't know how he'd awake, but when he did, he ran from us, clearly afraid. He went all the way down the corridor to the front door on shaky legs. There he sniffed, frightened, under the door at the threshold. From there he ran past us again, still on shaky legs, to the back door and gave it the same inspection. What happened next disturbs me to this day. He slowly approached us, ears flat, and sniffed every inch of my hand. He moved to my other hand and then to my mouth. Carefully, he smelled my lips, my nose and chin. With a satisfied but still unsure huff, he moved to Sunny and repeated the entire process. We tried to calm him, but he spent the remainder of the dark hours alert, eyes trained on the front door. Like a parent, I'm sure, we wish to shelter our innocent charges from everything frightening, real or imagined, and we are heartsick when we encounter a fright we cannot dismiss. I can still only guess at the horror of Leppy's dream. Did we hurt him, or others hurt us?

ꝰ ꝰ ꝰ ꝰ

Boundless optimism greeted the first full day. I continued to feel awkward using anything but "puppy" to address him, but that would change as his unique characteristics grew into his unique name. Leporello is a stage name, the sidekick of Don Juan who wants nothing more than to be the boss. These are the opening lines to Mozart's *Don Giovanni,* and the confidence level of the puppy made this a fine choice. The couple who first took him home titled him Macbeth, but such a tragic figure suited our dog not the least. This Sunday morning meant a walk around the block, with its first sights and smells of sidewalk trees, of travertine stoops and of shadowy setbacks with garage doors. But he had no idea what excitement awaited him at home that afternoon. We had organized a homecoming party with some friends. They came over, and one by one ogled the adorable puppy – for Airedale puppies are irresistibly cute. They are born all black, and slowly, as they grow, have tawny patches inch their way over the chest, up the legs from the paws, and most winningly of all, from the outer edge of the ears inward. The effect on the ears is particularly unique, and looks like a silky black mohair cravat, neatly triangled, and edged in amber-gold thread.

We assembled on the front room floor, and there the puppy was passed around from hand to hand, from lap to lap, each new guest presenting a treat or new toy to bolster his collection of one. When David Franklin arrived, he joined the confabulation with something hidden from puppy's view behind his back. When the young pup was duly in David's lap, everything else came to a halt, for seemingly from the thin air, a snorting honk arose.

Puppy froze, ears and eyes at full alert as out came a stuffed hedgehog from behind David's back. Leporello blinked and divided his glance from brown furry thing to David's eyes. "Is that for me?" he asked as David held it to puppy's mouth – but before he surrendered it, David gave it a good squeeze. Out roared a sound akin to an *il basso* grunting and squealing at the same time. Leppy started and made a squiggle motion in David's lap, but in the next instant the hedgehog was in his mouth. The same sound came again, the same momentary squiggle, but this time David reacted, startled. In the sheer joy of the moment, a bit of momentary bladder control lapsed, and a piddle spot was joyously deposited on David's black denim. David laughed, and amid a riotous chorus of grunting squeaks, so did we all.

It was a wonderful time to be a puppy, for toy-wise, the market was suddenly awash with the new generation of squeakers and squawkers and snorters. These plush toys with built-in voices made my humble mouse, with its single small squeak, seem even more old fashioned than it was. Toys teach dogs, but also dogs with toys teach us about them. A short time later I found a hot-pink monkey in the pet store. Its internal voice was far different from the grunty squawk that was typical. This one, when squeezed, positively screamed – piercing and manic in direct relation to the pressure exerted. I bought it, but could not have imagined how it would deepen my understanding of who Leporello was as 'a person.' I was on the floor, gave it to him, and after his first squeeze, he dropped it in horror. "I've hurt it . . . . "

When he looked at me, his eyes were so pure, so filled with worry for the hot-pink monkey, that I can still see them now. I assured him, by saying in a high-pitched and silly voice (another gem from the 'puppy books'), that everything was all right. I picked up the toy and squeezed it a few times myself. After several nervous blinks, he loosened up a bit and took it lightly in his mouth. After a few moderate squeezes of his own, he seemed reassured. As he relaxed and began to play, I came to the profound realization that this little one was born gentle – a gentility, with which when I look to compare to my own, I find far superior every time.

The boundless optimism that seems the birthright of every puppy is something I sadly miss in my own nature today. We have Masetto, a nine-month-old Airedale puppy, but in that he is his own dog; he *is* quite a bit different from a puppy named Leppy. He confirms for me that Leporello's remarkable attributes were his and only partially attributable to his remarkable breed. Masetto has many fine and developing strong points, in fact he has many fewer head-strong negative ways than the nine-month old Leppy had, but still, they are different – and that is the way it should be. Too often we are told dogs are all alike, but in my experience, people are sadly more true to type than our canine fellow travelers. And yet still, Masetto's optimism is what I need, and quite frankly, it sustains myself in current times. Worries persist. Is Masetto safe, is he going to slip his leash and run into traffic, and on and on. Worries for us, in addition to worries for him.

With Leporello, at the end of fifteen and half years of life together, and of living with anxieties about him ever-present on my mind – does he have water, food; enough challenges and time to play with others; is he sick but I cannot tell – and oddly enough, at least for me anyway, I wondered for fifteen years and more if Leppy was happy. Was he content with us and the city life we led? Wasn't there a better family somewhere else, where he'd be better contented?

The day he died, the foremost obstacle in my path, the looming shadowy menace in my way forward, was a mindset of dull nagging guilt. For all those years, every memory casting back over every day was dusted with the thought of him and his well-being – and sadly, a day arrives where any random tomorrow means he exists not even one more day in it. The back-burner pot of logic feebly simmers. It tries to steam a certain softness with weak-as-water platitudes – he lived a long life; he was *not* alone when he drew his last breath; he *was* with his family – but the forefront pain only knows one all demanding phrase – he is gone. It leaves for me no space without the anxiety of his everyday well-being, but the bare starkness of my own anxieties of separation, of my own doubts, of my own lonesomeness.

ఌ ఌ ఌ ఌ

On the evening of that first Sunday, walking around the block, we encountered a setback for one of those ubiquitous San Francisco garage doors. Because the full side of the neighboring building came out to the sidewalk, a mini vortex would sometimes arise. This day, the dried and fallen – but still beautifully crimson – petals of the bougainvillea growing next to the garage door were puddled in the driveway. As we came by, a gust of wintry wind swirled in the garage niche and picked up the flower petals into a sparkling tornado. Leppy jumped right into the middle of it as carefree as a kid jumping into a ball vat. He glanced at me momentarily, like he was wondering why I didn't join him in the midst of so much fun. At the moment, mine were the worries; his was the pure unalloyed fun of living full in the present. He invited me, but could I not go? Sadly, no.

But as I stood there and watched, I felt that this young dog, whether he lived long or short, would like nothing so much as to be hoisted by the wind, and spun with the red papery triangles as far up as they could carry him. [5]

ESSAY III:
Springtime in the Park

In one of my high school American Literature classes, Sister Elaine Freund gave us broad analogies for Hawthorne's brilliant novel *The Scarlet Letter*. The color white, she told us, Hawthorne used to designate pure and good; black, was suspicious and doleful. She pointed out how Hester was often couched in white or off-white language, and Dimmesdale, via his very name, was often mired in inklike self-broodings. One day, after she had moralistically hinted that the daughter of their illicit union was murky in sin because of her birth, I raised my hand and dared to point out that Hawthorne had named this daughter "Pearl." Hawthorn had titled this char-acter after nature's purest white. In several scenes, like the one where she sits in her father's lap, Hawthorn drenches Pearl, and the people she touches, in radiant sunlight. Indeed it seems Pearl is the only one who brings some cleansing warmth to Dimmesdale's self-tortured heart. Surely, I dared to assert to Sister Elaine, Pearl is a statement of nature's absolute innocence; absolving in its very presence any taint or mark, visible or deeply buried. So too was Leporello – a nature dog of anti-apathetic-crushing boldness, a personality who put others at ease via the very ease which he had for himself, and with the world he seemed to run.

Our puppy, freshly installed in our lives, daily grew stronger and more confident. As Teddy Roosevelt sated it, "An Airedale can do anything any other dog can do, and then lick the other dog, if he has to." [6] This judicious restraint of kingly power is well suited for city settings. The open-eyed puppy assessment of all expressions of joy from Sunny and me, and from the myriad people he chanced to meet, he internalized to an outward *joie de vivre*. The walks to one of the many parks near our house – Duboce, Buena Vista, Corona Heights – always meant making friends, as people were helplessly drawn to his adorable face and smiling tail. It's hard to think of a time when Leppy did not 'own' the crowd of canines who greeted his park entry with an eager flocking around him. Like a canine Good Shepherd, he let the little ones come to him with jiggly backsides and sniffing fronts. Leporello would stop stiff-legged, head erect, but for all who knew him, this was a show, his *nom de jeu,* his calling card by which he boldly made his first assessment of any dog's willingness to play. His system worked like this: pose with stance stiff and still; give a moment for the other dog to sniff; then meet them eye to eye; pause. This was followed in quick succession by an inexplicably energetic lunge to the side away from the other dog. The play aspect of this jog to the side was usually hammered home with a quick bobbing of the head, bent elbows, and the front paws patting the ground. Sometimes the other dog would start at the sudden bolt and retreat, in which case Leppy let them pass; or the other dog would become aggressive and bad tempered. They'd snarl and yap; maybe take a step towards Leppy, but he'd never be led into ill will, and would simply leave them cold in their dead-end humor. But the third kind, the 'correct' reaction that Leporello lived for, was a dog who instantly responded to his play with like kind; the ones who, watching Leppy's joyful gavotte, followed after him with their own. Then the two would be off in a running exploration of the sunshine world of the parkland together. Countless are the dogs our growing pup enchanted with his greeting dance.

Much can be taught from dog to person or from person to dog. But by far the most information any dog gets on dogliness comes from other dogs. One day Leppy was with a few roving pals in the leaf-littered undergrowth of the trees that mark the edges of Corona Heights Park. Leppy was sniffing something while a random dog lingered close by, in fact, right in front of him. Without warning, that dog stiffened his legs, and scissor-like, scratched the fallen eucalyptus leaves and bark strips. This debris hit Lep straight in the face and startled him. Intrigued however by what had happened, he stuck by this dog until he did it again. This time the Airedale observed carefully the form of the other, and at the third scratching display, Leppy stiffened his own legs and joined in. "This is fun. This is a release of pent up frustrations." And this was a permanent new behavior passed from one canine to another.

ॐ ॐ ॐ ॐ

He grew. That was beyond our guidance, but he grew mentally and emotionally stronger too. How do parents raise children, how do adoptive dog parents raise puppies that are true nature-beings, expressions of the best of dogged optimism? How to raise a perfectly well-natured, well-adjusted individual when you lack these attributes yourself? The answer is – he raises you. Nature in its pure form can easily deal with unstable inconsistencies. I speak for and of myself, for while my foibles are nearly legion – short in patience, often myopic and afflicted with forest-for-the-trees syndrome – his virtues trumped those of nearly every saintly man and woman. He was patient to a fault, generous, non-passive, and most non-human of all, a truly non-conceited, non-judgmental receiver of love.

As we gathered on a clear November day to celebrate his first birthday, we were proud. Puppy had raised us well, and as beaming acolytes, Sunny and I planned an appropriate party. Several dogs were invited to our house: there was the black Cocker Spaniel, Betsy, and the other Airedale of the neighborhood, Jackson, to name but two. Jackson was a well-loved dog by his two moms, but he, about 6-months older than Lep, was a problem. He was insecure and developed into a paranoid adolescent. That day at the party, I recall looking into his eyes and thinking he was only partially with us; the other focus of his attention was absorbed by phantom sights, sounds and smells. At that moment, the doctor in me thought Jackson most probably suffered from a form of clinical schizophrenia, despite the no-doubt loving environment his parents provided him with at home. I believe nowadays, vets prescribe "people meds" to dogs to help with the outward signs of this condition – a condition prevalent in some breeds, mostly in Dalmatians, but unfortunately also to some degree in Airedales. In 1996 though, such treatment was still unheard of.

In the park, people would often become rigid at the first sight of Leppy, calling out to us "Jackson?" "Leppy!" we would reply, and they instantly relaxed the collars of the dogs they were holding back. One time a young German Shepherd attacked our angel. Leppy would have made Teddy Roosevelt proud, for he held his own; was neither hurt, nor hurt the attacker before the Shepherd's owner pulled the aggressor off. We later learned that this dog had been bullied and bitten by Jackson when a pup.

At the party, an Alpo cake, made canned dogfood, was greeted all around, even by the taciturn Jackson, with happy abandon. At the end of the day, Leppy lay amid a sea of new toys like a Roman Emperor just stepped from his treasure bath. His canvas mouse, now with one chewed ear, rested unceremoniously at the bottom of his toy chest. Sitting there, I reached a hand to Sunny. How lucky were we? Fate, with her thrice-told 'almosts,' had moved much to allow us to raise him, and he to raise us.

ट ट ट ट

I have often thought, even the average dog makes a better person than the most saintly of our own kind; their run-of-the-mill betters our stamped-in-gold. This acceptance of fact leads to the realization that there are some things in the soul that need a proper airing once in a while. These are like sheets set on a line to be bleached naturally by the sun – disinfected by the Sol of the Lysol brand. *When* we take out our neatly folded and tightly packed linen is a random guess, because the scheduling works on a timeframe devised by others. When we chance to meet someone whom we feel lives better than we do – by better, I mean more wholly, more connectedly to their environment or to themselves – *then* we are forced to shake out the bugaboos of our own character and hang them out for neighbors and ourselves to see.

That Leporello was a nature-boy should not be a surprise anyone. But that he was a pure expression of the noblest unnatural – that is, of unself-advantageousness – should surprise. For we are taught that Nature is a dumb, greed-handed brute, and that a dog-eat-dog world exists save for the re-deeming grace of mankind and the fragile society we have built up. But, what a peccadillo of deception this belief is. Pearl in Hawthorne's world is the absolved one. She is Nature referred to without sin, and if her parents could shed the blinders of social self-hate, they too would see this, and they could forgive themselves too. On a personal level, the truth of the matter embarrasses me to say, but Leporello was a better person than I am. Freer, more connected both to himself and to others than I feel I can yet achieve in the life left to me. Even though, enlightened as I seem to be, at least to myself, I cannot seem to find the way back into being the faultless Nature-child that was Leppy's joyous birthright.

ESSAY IV:
Disaster Dog / Devil Dog

I may be only half as patient as I pretend, to paraphrase the Earl of Sandwich (Yes, that Earl of bread-and-roast-beef Sandwich fame!) who once declared himself to be only half as wicked as he acted, and said it to the Devil no less, or at least to someone he believed to be the Devil. But for me, patience is a challenge. I gradually watched the Bambi-eyed wonder of our beloved pet gradually give way to a mastery of confidence as our adolescent pup grew. In those eyes too appeared a certain calculation: punishment versus impulse-reward. The gears turned behind those windows of his soul, and we often termed our teenage companion canine a Devil Dog. Many are the times that the in-between child and adult dog pulled me over my unsteady edge, as the one time in the Marin Headlands where he actually did pull me over an eight-foot embankment to go crashing to the dirt road below on my knees; and many are the sad regrets that my chastisements were too strongly rough. But that visible flicker of mental function, as seen via the sparkle of the eyes, weighed the calculus of fleeting reward versus the punishment. When, however, what he wanted to do – run out into the street for example – was a threat to his health, I, despite my best efforts at neutrality, once the dust settled down, found myself in admiration of his spirit. His devilish reasoning ability conflated fair with unfair.

Examples of the worst sort are these: once while we were stopped at a red light, he jumped out the car window. Now, you probably think to yourself, the window was open? Well, yes, but only a quarter of the way down. How he scrambled through without breaking it, I shall never know. Fortune allowed that I was holding onto the leash when he bailed out, so he couldn't run off through the intersection, and into traffic.

His first Easter, about four or five months old, he climbed

on a Hitchcock chair to get at the table holding our Easter basket. We found it later, shredded, the paper grass spread to every corner of the house, and the marshmallow chicks and chocolate bunny eaten with most with its foil still attached. I know. Now you are saying that we left chocolate within the dog's reach . . . but for this tyke to get to the tabletop required a Herculean effort, and like Laddie Boy fetching a golf ball from a tree, took an engineering mind. We learned a valuable Airedale lesson – nothing is beyond their will. With them, as Billy Shakespeare said, all things be ready if the mind be so. However, that was only the opening volley in that day's disasters, for perhaps the elusive non-digestible element in the chocolate, or just a plain old-fashioned sugar rush caused our dear Leporello to proceed to chew the entire side rail off of the accomplice Hitchcock chair, then to go willfully to the other side of the table – to the other companion Hitchcock chair – and go after its leg. Not satiated, he proceeded to gnaw on three corners of the treat-hosting table. Note: he must have been standing on the chairs to reach these corners . . . so he must have done these first.

I believe this time marked the one and only instance when Leppy 'talked back' to me as he was being punished. Our method was this – he was sent to the back room, either he went on his own, following my pointed finger, or I firmly applied my grip to his collar and led him there. There he'd get a dressing down. On this occasion, prompted by the inadvertently harassing tatters of an Easter basket in my waving hand, or the aforementioned lack of enzymes to digest the chocolate – or, an abundance of sugar, or I know not which – he cracked. The usual humility he suffered during these punishments was shown by remorsefully bent ears and lowered eyes, but this time, halfway through, he glowered sharply at me and slowly, a low rumbling growl sounded from under his breath. This surprised me, but emotions took over and I heard myself yell so loudly in response to his murmur that he instantly crumpled to the floor. He never growled at me, or indeed at anyone, ever again in his life.

ॐ   ॐ   ॐ   ॐ

The question in my mind is how do you learn the concept of unfairness? Did Leppy react as he did from the function of being, in his mind, unfairly punished? In the fourth grade, our teacher had a sort of tribunal system for minor in-class infractions. The accused was formally arraigned by a witness, or the teacher, and a group of students heard testimony and decided on exoneration or a fitting punishment. Once I was accused and found guilty of something Joey did. What, I do not recall, but as no tattle-tale, I kept the truth to my defenseless self. The punishment was for me to extend my arms and hold several encyclopedia volumes level for the entire ten minutes of recess. Bitter was the experience – the physical pain, the accentuator of psychological injustice.

Real injustice though was on display in Duboce Park; inequities that punished the canine victims more than their human tormentors. There was a man, say in his 50s, who had the sweetest and most demure rottweiler. This dog would run and cavort with all the other dogs in brilliant fellowship, that is, after he received his daily 'training' from the man. This man arrived at the park not to let his canine buddy socialize, but to control-freak the dog into a sitting position and lock his eyes onto every whim of his 'master.' He trained this companionable dog – there in the open, public fresh air – with the German words for "at-tack," "bite," "don't let go," and would extend his padded arm to force the dog to attack him. The end of this dog's fable is that one fine day he attacked his owner severely, then killed a small dog and viciously bit the woman shielding her Maltese. The real victim, the rottweiler, was lethally-injected by the Humane Society; the real criminal, the man, was ticketed and seen in the park in a couple of weeks 'training' a German Shepherd puppy. Another was a twenty-something hipster fond of wearing a knitted cap all year round, including in the height of summer. He had armfuls of tattoos and many more holes in his head that God originally gave him. This guy also had a smaller-sized Staffordshire Terrier mix, but his dog was allowed to play, was well-socialized, and a favorite among the human visitors to the play field. In short, the dog was evidently well looked after and loved. After a few days of noted absence from the scene, this dog reappeared in the park barely able to walk. The problem was between his front legs – his entire chest and neck had been shaven and was painfully red and swollen. This red irritation and swelling made it uncomfortable for him to walk, and impossible for him to frolic. But why was it swollen? Mr. Knit Cap had tattooed the entirety of his dog's chest in a sunburst pattern. The result: the dog was 'rescued' by being cage-isolated in the pound, while the man was wrist-slapped. Two examples of sweet dogs mangled on the rocks of human caprice.

ẽ   ẽ   ẽ   ẽ

As for Leporello's other Devil Dog examples, there are many; like the time he ran four blocks out of the park to chase down a particular Chow Chow he was in love with. But dogs' errant ways are nothing if not pure unalloyed expressions of Nature. So different are they from Man's embodiment of evil avarice – by which I mean, not merely dumb open-handed greed, but man-style plotting and scheming to rob others of their fair share. The real name for the deadly sin is avarice; 'greed' is a dull stand-in.

It's ironic schools fail to quantify traits like these in their young charges. For recent news of an innovative measure of IQ, or rather of a refinement on how to assess it, has come to light. The concept is referred to as Emotional Intelligence (which is also called EQ, or a person's Emotional Quotient.) Standardized IQ testing does not change, but predictions of future well-being are tested for in children via the EQ method. A classic example: kids are given an ice cream cone. They are told to hold off eating it until the tester gives the signal. Then another person enters the room and whispers something in the ear of the tester and leaves. The tester tells the kids he must step out for a minute; the little ones can eat the ice cream if they want, but if they wait until he comes back, he will give them an additional treat. Those who are unable to wait will get the cone in their hand but nothing more. The EQ theory holds that the kids who can focus on the future, despite the temptation and reward of instant gratification, will be more likely to develop into contented adults. The theory says they will also be better able to utilize their grownup Intelligence Quotient.

I wondered about this in regards to the child I was, and incredibly, I had a parallel ice cream example, though not an exact match. One hot day when I was five – it must have been in late September, for the school-aged kids were not around – Marian, the young mother of five children who looked after me mornings and afternoons, said she could bear the heat no more and packed me off with her to the frozen treat kiosk at the public pool. Marian bought two cones, one for herself and one for me, but insisted we wait until we got back home to eat them. She said I could watch *Flipper* instead of her daily 3 PM soap if I waited and held her cone for her while she drove. [7] So there I sat – in the back seat of their family's mid-1970s LTD, in heat well over ninety degrees, my sweaty legs sticking to the vinyl below my Bermuda shorts – with towering ice cream cones propped in both hands. Even with the windows down, the back of the sedan was like an oven, and Marian drove through the back streets of town like a bat out of hell. [8] She took corners so sharply that I was toppled over onto my elbow. Had I not been sweat-glued to the plastic upholstery, I would have slid across that great sofa of a back seat to the other side. I tried to hold the cones upright, I tried to focus on which way to adjust for the upcoming turn, but my sight was obscured by Marian's shoulders, and consequently there was more ice cream to vinyl contact than was warranted. Safely parked at home, she opened the back door and glowered at the mess. Not only was there ice cream deposited on the seat and side of the car door, but there was also some on the back of the front seat (did I mention the brake-slamming?). And me, I sat still with more of the sticky stuff oozing down the length of arms and hands, from the tips of my elbows to the top and sides of my legs. "Why didn't you lick some?" she demanded to know. "You told me to wait" was my only defense.

🐚 🐚 🐚 🐚

Perhaps not meaning to, the effect was that Marian punished me for doing what she had asked, and sadly introduced me to my first taste of injustice. Perhaps it's inevitable that as parents we come to these moments, and with Leppy I was the first who watched his bright eyes sink when I unwittingly dealt him his initial blow of this miserable feeling. I had played with him, taking up one of his toys from the floor and hugging it close to my chest saying "Mine." He'd come over, try to take it, etc. We'd play, but the clarity of "mine" in Leppy's mind solidified in my brain as I was snacking on something. He sat before me, looking to partake of whatever it was I was enjoying. On a spur of the moment – an evil spur of ill-conceived conceit – I clutched the food to my chest and said the dreadfully inappropriate word "Mine." His expectant ears went limp, and the jollity of his sparkle blinked a single sad hurt. A sense of injustice, a sense of what human avarice looks like, slackened his jaw and cracked open his face. This is the precise moment he learned what "unfair" meant; what capricious greed looks like in the face of openness; and I had taught it to him.

ESSAY V:
❧ Walks With Leporello

I suppose there is something in the very act of walking that engenders reflection. The heart beats along as we go, the limbs chug, nicely circulating the life force, and we become connected with the now in a way that our brains alone can never be. While we walk, we are simultaneously settled with the present and keep pace with what has gone before. The future, that is left to the side when we are really trekking along, and that condition is for the most part a relief to us. The body soothes the mind. But it's also true that memories – nostalgia – keep pace with where we look and what we see. A building where we had friends live; a set of terrazzo steps where we are forced to pause; or a blooming iris that takes one to the scent of many springs past. These reminders seem to potential themselves with every footfall.

There is something of the tinge of heavy nostalgia resting on carefree Airedale shoulders. Any number of people we chanced to meet during our walkabouts bore witness to this. Leppy brought out – what I like to think of as – a far-away look of remembrance in some people. It should not be surprising that so many individuals have been touched by the breed, because as you cast back through the generations, Airedales will become more and more prevalent. It is only natural that America's one-time Number One most popular breed should continue on in many peoples' power of recollection. There also seems to be a shared memory, whether engendered from personal contact or not, of the Airedale's traits of smarts and bravery. And why not? When Americans themselves were bolder, they kept bolder dogs to be the quintessential All-American mascot – Airedales per-fectly fit the bill for the optimistic 1920s, and were for them the Golden Retrievers of our tuned-out, sleepier day.

As for Leporello, after turning the corner of his one-year mark, the adolescent "I can't be bothered" steeliness of his glint slowly gave way. It returned to his puppyhood's non-judgmental gazes. I like to fancy he slowly grew to understand that, for one, he could hurt himself with some of his impulse decisions, and two, that we would always be there to comfort that ouchy paw he raised for our inspection. We, as the mouse, could Aesop-fashion remove the thorn from between our mighty lion's tender toes.

ॐ   ॐ   ॐ   ॐ

Leppy went out morning and evening on his constitu-tionals; Sunny taking the morning shift, and I the evenings. We'd always meet members of the diverse crowd that peopled our neighborhood. Duboce Triangle is like the over-lapping sheet corners of surrounding districts. It seems that several 'halves' meet on common ground to live in the Triangle. Half are Gay folk from the Castro, half Latino from the Mission; half are working class from the Western Addition, and half are moneyed easy-streeters from the Corona Heights and Buena Vista enclaves. It's a melting pot with a gentle, sweet savor from the few old-timers born there, or moved there just after the war. These were mostly ladies, in their 70s and 80s, whom I'd meet gaily folding their laundry next to us apartment-renters at the laundromat. I'd also meet them chatting with the proprietors of the corner groceries. Very happy souls, they always had a warm smile and open, soft-reaching hands for Leppy and me. Encouragement and optimism were the lifeblood of their generation.

There was also a small proportion of Vietnam Vets, like our next-door neighbor, who would carry his geriatric dog up and down the steps of his building's stoop. The man got a young companion dog from the SPCA who was the very model of patience. This young dog would pace his youth to wait for the elder dog on their walks, and because of it, he slowly lost all the looks of youth. His coat became thin, his shoulders and neck stooped, and his eyes obtained a far-away look, gazing intently as they did on his human companion to tell him if was going too fast. One day, the elder dog passed away. Slowly, walk by walk, the young dog shook away the fetters of slowness like a child shedding the trappings of mourning garb. His eyes took on a new cast, and he now looked with glee upon every encouragement from the man he walked with. He explored new nooks, new trees and his tail rose to a prominent position of confidence and joy.

Step and eyes brightened, his coat thickened and glossed, and the spots of hairlessness from the elder's affliction of mange disappeared. This rebirth was complete when the veteran brought home a new puppy. Now the young dog was a young parent, and to complete the arc of his growth, he could turn his quiet deferential love to an active ardor. He seemed to me like a butterfly cracking his chrysalis.

ॐ ॐ ॐ ॐ

For people in general, walking is a way to make time to tune out, but for dogs, it's a time for all senses to be reporting to the processing centers of the brain at full force. Bored at home, to be able to smell something challenging – something natural – is a stimulating relief to canines. For the longest time I wondered in frustrated impatience why, after sniffing a tree for a long time and then raising his leg upon it in benediction, Leppy would often insist on turning right back to the same spot and sniff it in slow contemplation for a second or third time. But looking at it through his eyes, or rather, smelling it through his nose, I realized his concentration was applied to one thing – deciphering one scent. This item analyzed, he went back to process the next piece of information, and on and on. I figured this out through applying the same logic to my listening to a friend's voice in a noisy restaurant. The muzak, the silverware clatter, all is cut out, but if I wanted to eavesdrop to the neighboring table, I could focus on that other voice with no problem. People who did not know him, or his sense of humor, may find this hard to believe, but sometimes when my impatience manifested itself with a gentle tug of the leash away from a thirdly inspected tree, Leppy would overreact and stumble back on the pavement like I had just yanked with all my might. He would, believe it or not, only do this when there was a person walking right past us at that moment. As this third party glared with hostile intent at the brute I was, Leppy would shoot a devil-dog "Serves you right" glance in my direction.

With dogs, so much information comes through the nose that the eyes are given second-class priority. Since all kinds of people were drawn to Leppy, I occasionally had to divert his attention onto a waiting admirer. This however was never especially true with children. Children presented their own unique challenges to me when walking, not because I didn't know what Leporello would do – as his kind actions were guaranteed to be straightforward – but because of the sheer unpredictability on the child's side. The best kind of youngster for him was one who just extended open arms for Leppy to walk into. He'd place his head literally in their hands to receive their gentle petting, and he'd turn his flank for them to reach their arms around his middle. By this time, usually a wide-eyed parent would yank the child by the other arm to disengage them. Their lesson about not every dog being as friendly as Leporello was a valid one. As for the myriad displays from average children – running, screaming in delight, or cowering, crying, or screaming in fright – they could all be seen, sometimes one right after the other. Leporello, for his part, was exemplary with children even from his youngest days. His approach was to mirror their actions towards him. He ignored children who ignored him; he acted fearful of those fearful of him; and was warm and generous with those of open smiles and beckoning hands. As I said, he would walk into their embrace, meet them eye to eye, and turn his body just right for a childish grasp to hug him in the most effective way.

As for adult encounters, often we met with people who grew up with this breed and would wax longingly over Leppy's visage and smiling tail. At other times, we'd encounter those who had some surprising intelligence to relay about Airedales. One fellow, wearing a camo jacket and looking a bit world-weary, stopped us. With some cautiously fleeting glances at the dog, he proceeded to relate how Airedales are fearless; how they died carrying messages between trenches in the Great War; and how they were the preferred weapon to hunt lions in Africa. "A gun with reasoning ability," he said, adding, "Air-dale – that's spelled E-I-R-E-Dale, right?" Not quite, but he later went on to mention he believed there was an Irish connection to the breed, which would explain his EIRE for Ireland. In the meantime, so engrossed was he in his information relay, that he failed to take any further notice of Leppy's presence. Eventually, bored because of the prolonged stop, Leppy sidled up to the man's knees, leaned on him and looked him in the eyes. This was Leppy's invite for a good long stroking session, but the man started at the physical contact with the "lion killer" and jumped to the side. In half an instant though, he looked with amazed eyes and asked me, "Is it all right . . . ?" He meant to pet Leppy, and I encouraged him whole-heartedly. In the moment after a tentative caress of his hand, Leppy's artless warmth prompted the man to genuflect and rub vigorously. Leporello, as "Thank you," gave him a quick lick on the face, and the man rose with a beaming smile as bright as the sun. The abstract made concrete; fearful tales of Airedales absolved by the loving blessing of one. "Go and sin no more," Leppy seemed to say.

Another time a woman stopped us. She was a slightly bedraggled baby boomer who told me she'd kept Airedales in the good old psychedelic days of the 1960s. "Butter," she advised in nervous earnestness. "They'll do anything you want for butter. Try it." She raised her eyebrows in a quick confidence and went her way. I puzzled for a moment there on the sidewalk and thought that Leppy probably had not ever tasted butter. So, that evening, after the walk, I pulled some out to see if Leporello would go wild for the good stuff. Regardless of it being laced with nothing hippier than a suspicion of salt, Leppy liked it, but appeared to me to be of the opinion that he could take it or leave it.

Coincidentally enough, just about this time, the November 1997 issue of *Food and Wine Magazine* arrived on my doorstep. I have said that everyone in the 1920s had Airedales, and Julia Child had been no exception. She provided a girlhood Thanksgiving memory set in Pasadena where she grew up. Their family Airedale Eric had caused a Turkey Day butter crisis. Little Julia's mother had set the table, including her special sterling silver individual serving butter plates. All the crystal was set; all the silverware and napkins had likewise been placed. Confidently knowing everyone preparing the dinner knew their role, she stepped out of the house for an errand. Coming back through the dining room to the kitchen, she immediately asked the maid why the butter had not been placed, and was told that the special holiday-mood curled portions had indeed been doled out. Standing dumbfounded over the immaculate table, the head scratching of the two women resolved nothing, until they heard a slightly scrambled sound from behind the living room sofa. "Eric!" they cried. Hearing his name, he dutifully presented himself, but with guilt-lowered ears. A cockeyed tilt of a picked-up butter plate to the light revealed clear tongue streaks. Even as Mother waved the silver plate accusingly under Eric's shiny black nose, she had to admire how the dog had gone from serving to serving, stretching his proboscis to snatch every last dreg of the solidified nectar. It's doubtful he appreciated that each portion had been formed into pretty little curls. But that he had done his pilfering without upsetting one piece of crystal, moving one plate or wrinkling a single napkin comes as no surprise to the experienced Airedale person. Eric for his part, even though he looked demure and regretful, had had a great Thanksgiving. The conversation sparked about him continued as the family sat down to view the dinner spread, and I suspect a certain little Julia gave him a little extra butter under the table, because life is short, as she'd often later say. [9]

Similarly, as in the kismet fashion of the 'butter connection,' a few years later we bought an unassuming book called *All About Airedales* in our new neighborhood. [10] This rare little gem was on decorous display in a pet boutique on Church Street. This store rounded out their off-the-shelf stock with one-off antiques that featured dogs or cats. This book, from 1911, for example, was open and standing next to a 1930s child's hanger with a cutesy-cutesy transfer of Scotties in mid frolic. Buying this tome, I learned that the author provided that exceptional and important California view of Airedales. Here in writing was proof of what someone long ago, perhaps even Leppy's breeder, had told me about Airedales. One of the purest stocks is found in the Sierra Nevada Mountains, the originals having left the Aire Valley of the English midlands only twenty or so years after the breed was settled. Their distinctive features being unalloyed intelligence and bearing meant that by 1910 Airedales were the aristocratic companion dog of choice, and two were First Class passengers on the Titanic, neither of whom survived. [11] The performance of this amazing breed on the battlefields of Europe catapulted their renown into people's hearts, and resulted in some unwanted pressure on breeders. With the sudden rise of Airedales from a very rare breed in 1917 to America's number one breed by 1920, many smaller terriers were tossed into the American kennels providing pups to an eager market. And lo and behold, we found a written reference to Airedales hunting lions! But not in Africa . . . more like Placer County, California. Page

122 of the book mentioned above, under the chapter called "Using Airedales to Capture Mountain Lions Alive," gives printed account of a grand chase and eventual tree-cornering of a pair of cougars; one nine-foot-long. Two photos on an earlier page show cougars run up trees so they could be captured unharmed. [12]

So it turns out, our sidewalk informant, the man in camo, got his facts correct, but his continents misplaced. [13]

On our walks, Leppy would make life-long friends at the slightest of provocations. Once we were crossing the street, and he glanced over his shoulder. Another man was crossing behind us, and Leppy insisted he knew him. We had to stop, Leppy lowered his ears and forced the man to stop and greet him. He was a good sport, and the dog was happy. On occasions like this I wonder if dogs do not sometimes suffer from cases of mistaken-smell-dentity? – that someone smells so similar to some-one else the dog knows, they mistake one for the other. It's merely speculation on my part, but it somehow seems plausible to me.

Another of Leppy's human "finds" of this nature was a man who lived around the corner. One evening as we were walking past, the door to his ground-level flat opened and he took a step out. Leppy insisted we stop, and the befuddled man – another good sport – had a new best friend for life. This was reinforced by the coincidence of the man being there occasion-ally as we walked by. I believe Leppy always knew when the door would open just for him.

Other Airedales may not have been lion hunters, but they were national figures. Teddy Roosevelt was the first White House resident to have one, or possibly several, but he was far from the last. [14] Woodrow Wilson had his Davie. [15] Calvin Coolidge's had two: Paul Pry and Laddie Buck. [16] And these be-loved pets formed a GOP presidential passing of the baton, because the first was brother to, and the second, son of, Warren Harding's Laddie Boy.

Of all the well-known Airedales in history, Laddie Boy is the best loved by memory. The First Dog of his nation, Laddie Boy won the hearts of millions with his nationally syndicated column – in which he talked about Harding's official doings in the White House – and the many photos of Laddie Boy jumping almost into the President's arms when the man came home from official business. The dog's love and devotion to the President was on international display, perhaps as a nothing-special type of love for an Airedale, but it was surprising in its degree to the average dog owner. Many are Laddie Boy's exploits, captured as they were by a press corps ostensibly there to follow Harding. Like the times Warren sliced golf balls into trees, and dutiful Laddie Boy scampered up the trunks and into the foliage to retrieve them. If you think this is easily accomplished for a dog, it is not, but an Airedale-mind-made is a match for all challenges.

News of the dog's premonition of the president's death in office added immensely to the national grief. Even though the President and First Lady had been gone for weeks on a trip to Alaska, Laddie Boy held down the White House fort with calm normality. This all changed when he inexplicably became agitated, stopped eating, and was prone to baleful howlings. Left to his own devices, he began to spend all of his time standing by a pair of French doors on the west side of the White House. A photographer captured his worried and far-sighted eyes looking to where the sun would set. All of this began and ended as the President lay dying in San Francisco. Seventy-two hours of Laddie Boy's restless agitation became quiet, numb grief at the moment of the man's passing on the other side of the continent.

Nearly 20,000 pennies were donated by children, Statue of Liberty fashion, to build a permanent memorial to Laddie Boy in the White House. Sculptor Bashka Paeff melted the pennies and rendered a life size bronze portrait to always stand guard in the People's House and be as loyal and loving to every forthcoming President as he had been to Warren G. Harding. Their dreams were altered by the whims of future trends, and Laddie Boy's statue was moved to the Smithsonian, where he is no longer on display. However, this is not the only memorial to Laddie Boy, as a beautiful stained-glass window in his native

Ohio also celebrates his life. And in many people's hearts he reposes comfortably with those who do not forget the service he faithfully rendered his country. [17]

(Photo Source: Library of Congress)

Laddie Boy, captured on the afternoon of August 1st, 1923, looking anxiously from inside the White House as the President lay dying in San Francisco. Warren G. Harding was to pass away in a matter of hours from the time this photo was taken. [18]

One 'command' I taught Leppy sometime when he was five or six years old was "Say Hello." The nose leads the way, and when the canine olfactory sense is engaged, concentration shuts down perception-processing from the other senses. It's the same with humans; when we read something, for example, noises become something easy to shut out. With Leppy, because of his size and beauty, people always wanted to pet him. If he was engaged in smell analysis, even though he was looking directly at someone, he'd miss the signs that they wanted to greet him. It dawned on me that if I let him know, he'd want to socialize. So "Say Hello" would instantly cause him to stop smelling, blink and look around for some warm-hearted, interspecies mingling.

In more current times, two moves later, our new neighborhood was much like the first. It had a mix of people – new-timers and old-timers together. On the corner lived a lovely Polish lady. Perhaps in her 70s, she always greeted the tail-wagging Leppy by getting on one knee and crooning low "I love you . . . I love you . . . " right into his ear. She'd hug him dearly, and he responded with deferential mannerisms and an upward gaze. She'd kiss his forehead.

One evening – a lucky evening for Lep – she emerged with a ziploc bag containing about half a pound of cooked pork chop pieces. She spoon fed him until I felt embarrassed and said she should keep some for other dogs. "But . . . *Kocham cię,*" she re-plied in Polish, all while Leppy dutifully emptied her bag one delicious morsel at a time. Other lucky sidewalk finds were not so enjoyable for him though. Many were the discarded drumstick bones that needed rescue, but I'd pry open his mouth and make him drop them. I came to realize that for him this was equivalent to me finding a perfectly good twenty-dollar bill on the sidewalk, and someone slapping it out of my hand. "Why?" his eyes would try to reason with me. "That was still good . . . . "

As for the dear lady, her very hugs were suffused with the sweet pangs of nostalgia. She told me how she'd come to this country after World War II, got a good manufacturing job and enjoyed dancing in the ballrooms of the old San Francisco she knew. "I used to raise Poodles," she told me confidentially, "and believe me"—said glancing over a shoulder—"dogs are better than people nowadays. Much better, like your angel!" And then to him, she'd add a soft, "I love you . . . . "

ॐ ॐ ॐ ॐ

A couple of weeks before he died, Leporello had his last warm encounter with a child. As we walked, a young South Asian couple with tot in stroller, purposefully crossed the street in front of us. Leppy was busy with the smells on a tree and did not notice them stop. I tapped him twice, my new signal for him to come along, since his hearing was almost all gone. He looked up, and when he did so, a pair of little arms extended from the stroller. The little attached hands wiggled slowly with open and beckoning fingers. Leppy walked right into that embrace. He placed his head on the little boy's lap as the child's mamma gave him his first lesson on how to gently stroke a dog's head. Leppy for his part, wagged a slow and supremely contented tail. Sad to say, but in these final few weeks, his tail-wagging became less and less, but as he was invited into an open-armed embrace, and his head petted by a little hand, his backside began to smile. I fancy in that quiet moment, where the current time was all-important, and the future forgotten, Leporello was overcome with the memories of the good old days. He was buoyed with the simultaneous pang of nostalgia and the warm and loving embrace of the present.

ESSAY VI:
Doe-Eyed Perseverance

VI. Doe-Eyed Perseverance 🐾

These are the eternal green pushings of youth –
rising impulses like the emerald-hued chlorophyll
in grass – they will grow despite less than ideal
conditions, placement or heritage. If we luxuriate
in life, we follow the original Latin meaning of the
word: we come to seed, to maturity, we have
made it out of vulnerable youth, and we can relax.
Past our purpose to reproduce an image of ourselves, we also proceed to deteriorate, or wither,
per the plant analogy. But at our back, it seems
eternal spring pushes us on to be young, to recall
the forces that governed our green haunts and
provided giddy pleasures in even the simplest
things – a hug from our parent, a kiss from our
first love, a jubilant feeling that time is on our side,
and that optimism is our natural bequest. So too
it was with our dear Leporello. Any of his youthful
wildness tamed down into calm self-awareness –
master of the park and sidewalk, Leppy had fear
for no situations, malice for no individual – even
those who hurt him like the Shepherd in the park
he seemed to pity – and he had strength to carry
less-than calm heads through every hairy situation
with aplomb.

His deep brown eyes stayed the same. Or, perhaps I should say,
they returned to their inherent serenity. The periodic flash of
challenge that would momentarily beset his look disappeared
with the end of his adolescence. Once again he regarded me with
the familiar and trusting eyes that remained the same from then
on. We have a picture taken on that first Sunday he was with us.
Sunny placed it in a frame where it has remained for fifteen
years. In the photo, the little twelve-week-old puppy is spread
half flat on the rug below me and the camera lens. His back legs
are flat and his two fore paws are quickly rising his front half.
His eyes, though, his eyes look at me through the camera with
his expression of supreme comfort; contentment with himself,
and with the young man standing before him. With this look is a

longing. A longing I have always known as one of wanting to connect – we are so different, people and dogs, yet they reach out to us with sweet understanding. I have many terms for those expressive eyes of Leporello – Bambi-eyes, Soul-seekers, and most commonly, I call them Mary-Pickford-eyes. That dear Canadian girl – America's Sweetheart – seems to have modeled her eye makeup on the Golden Retrievers of her day, because that same dark eye line lent her a patented Airedale sweetness. When we moved to the Noe Valley neighborhood in 1999, our still young dog seemed to have trouble adjusting. We lived out of boxes as I stripped the box beam ceiling, scraped the Mission Style brick mantelpiece, and he walked around with heart-break eyes. Remarkably, I was able to capture a photo of this miserable and pleading look of his. Remarkable because we have almost never been able to capture a non-red-eye picture of his Bambi-browns. When this photo came from the printers, I was set back on my heels at how clearly it captured this time in his life. It shows his ears wrenched back and flat on his head, while his eyes speak a milk-chocolate-sadness, humbly asking me to put the camera down and take him home. How to explain to him that this was our "new home," though absent from Duboce Park and our lovely ash-tree lined Noe Street, this new house and street and parkland offered just as much as 'home.' Finally the box beams were refinished, the bookcases in place and the dozens of boxes emptied onto their shelves. This room was done, and I unrolled the rug. Now this rug proved to be a bit special to Leppy because it came from our old front room. A room that for Leppy was out of bounds, unless we were with him. The unrolling of this rug proved to be a cornerstone for Leppy, for as I undid it, he was right by my side inspecting every freshly uncovered part with his nose. When the rug was laid flat, he gave it another complete circuit, ensuring every square inch of this familiar object was there, and then he turned to me, and plopped down with an immense relief-filled sigh. The rug communicates what I cannot – we *are* home; wherever *we* are together, we are *home.* This fact was borne out by our next move. When we came to our current house and neighborhood in 2003, Leppy relished the change and eagerly awaited the moment for the official rug unrolling. Then he repeated his inspection; he turned around and looked to me with the same comforting plop and sigh. For him, that was the moment we moved into our new home.

In Noe Valley, as I had been trying to tell him he might, he found a new love. The beautiful yet coy Chow Chow of his Duboce Triangle dreams stayed in his heart (no doubt), but around the corner from us now lived a striking Husky girl. She batted her blue eyes at him and drove him wild. She had white and warm-gray bushy fur and a face round as a sunflower, as indeed Chow Chows do. She'd flirt with Leppy in the most out-rageous way. She'd be sitting on the sidewalk with her human companion as he chatted to a neighbor and would pretend to not quite see us coming. I'd have to cross the street, but the vixen glance she'd toss at Leppy was accompanied by a cock of the head. A fervent look from Leporello to me, pleading for a closer meeting, was met with an "out of the question" finality on my part. Chicken bones, twenties, flirts on the sidewalks – my reactions and denials to all were unfair. His mini run for the hills after the Chow Chow left Duboce park had made me wary, but still I longed for Leppy, at least once, to encounter the Chow-Husky dream face in the flesh and act out the need to reproduce the beauty of himself with another. But children for him never happened, not for the want of us reaching out to Airedale breeders, but Leppy's offspring were all the children and humans that he touched perfectly with his heart.

ৡ ৡ ৡ ৡ

At the news of his demise, a certain little boy named Ren was deeply hurt. It touched my heart that an eight-year-old boy who encountered Leppy perhaps half a dozen times in his life would feel the loss so personally. A few years ago we held an Easter egg hunt for Ren and a few others of similar age. The morning of the hunt turned up raining, so I was forced to hide the decorated eggs in the house. As I had my basket, Leppy's nose was curious at its contents. He followed me around, step by step, as I placed the eggs – under the clock, behind the chest, here and there at each hiding place – Leppy followed with a deep sniffing confirmation. A gentle telling not to take them was all I needed to do. Dogs take the eccentricities of man with resigned ama-zement. I think of Jack London who said that dogs have a way of looking at people with a fine admixture of wonder and contempt: wonder that we can do so much; contempt that we actually do so little. If I suddenly took to placing cooked and dyed chicken eggs around the house, Leppy could forgive me and move on. When the hunt began, a light clicked in Leppy's head. I had done this strange thing for the little ones. Their hands groped here and there, between the chest and the wall, behind open doors, and Leppy was right there with them. Seeing the little hands grasp baskets like the one I'd used, he followed in their wake, confirming that they had obtained the hidden egg. And regarding one particular little girl, who was younger and less capable of finding the treats amidst the crowd of raucous boys, Leppy took her in hand, so to speak, and personally led her around – she instantly understanding his intent – and showed her where to look. Later, the end of the day found me a weary seeker of any errant ovum, but again Leppy came to the rescue. Starting exactly where I had started hours earlier, he led me one by one through all of my hiding places – sequentially – sniffing each cranny and looking up at me when he found an egg the kids had missed. Thank goodness, for there were at least three potential stink bombs I might not have disposed of otherwise. That night Leppy's Easter dinner was rich with reward in the form of chopped eggs.

A short time after this we began to want a companion for our dog. A gentle cur who could function as Leppy's pet during the weekdays. Sunny had a Cocker Spaniel when a little boy and we settled on that breed. Little Figaro, born in 2008, came from Oroville, which is a much farther drive than Sacramento had been all those years ago. We drove up there insistent upon finding a dog with Leppy criteria: about ten to twelve weeks old, and one who had grown up with his parents and siblings. There were two little boys available, their three sisters having already been placed, and we focused in on the little and gentle runt. He looked and acted very companionable. The long drive home followed the newly cemented 'old tradition' of the pup sitting on our lap. Mostly I drove and puppy curled on his towel in Sunny's well-contented grasp. After five hours of driving, we were finally home. I held the puppy under my left arm as I unlocked the front door. What happened next will probably always be my strongest memory of Figaro, for in the twilight house Leppy appeared from the kitchen and walked towards me at the door. The Cocker in my arm instantly stiffened. I glanced down to see him craning his neck and bobbing his head like an owl fixing his eyes on some far-off prey. The very instant Figaro was sure Leppy was a fellow canine, I felt Fig's stumpy tail begin to pound

Bean Bag Pile Up

Abby Gail

Sunny with Max –
Parakeet Cage in the Corner

Small Puppy in a Big World –
First Full Day Home

First Picture of Leppy at Home

The Dreaded Fire Hydrant

Sunny begging for . . .

A kiss – Marin Headlands

Leppy running free at Ocean Beach

Four months old –
In my arms on Corona Heights

Family portrait, Corona Heights

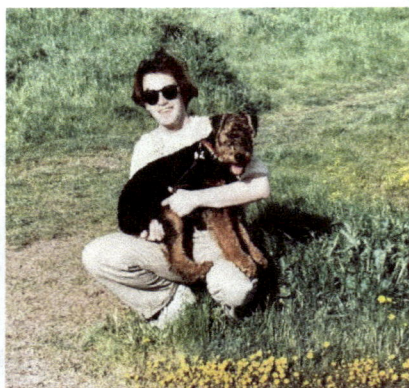
More fun on Corona Heights

Christmas 1996 – His first

Leporello's first tennis ball?

Christmas 1997 – "Bah, Humbug!"

Two years old –
He posed so nicely for me

Big and Beautiful

Leppy loved his toys

Summer of 1999

Summer of 2006

"Milk-Chocolate Sadness" –
Summer of 1999

On his front porch – 2007

Sunbathing on back deck

Figaro

Summer of 2008

Leporello and Figaro

In the back garden –
Summer of 2009

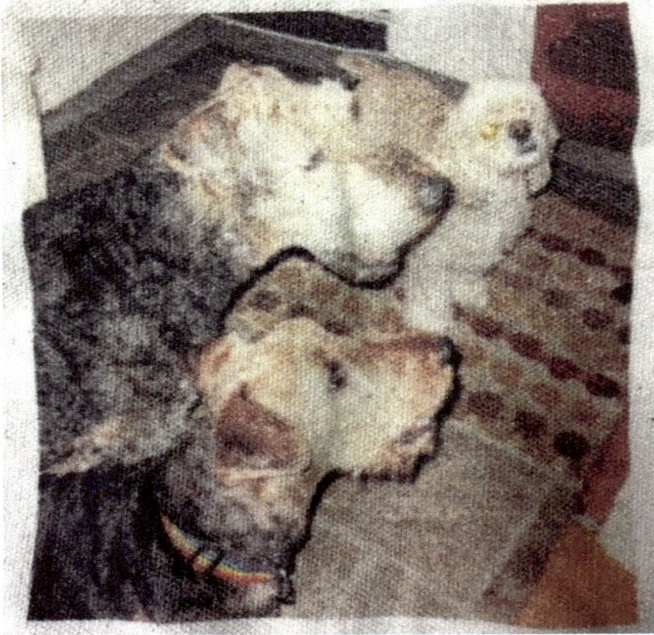

Masetto, Leporello and Figaro – 2010

Autumn of 2009

Ocean Beach – December 2010

the inside of my arm, and the outside flank of my side, with such vigor it went straight into my long-term memory. How happy he was. He squiggled his back legs excitedly and I set him down. In mid-run, he leapt towards the bemused Airedale and jumped on the other's terrier face with tiny front paws, looking for all the world to be indulging in playful laughter. Leppy did his park pose, but the puppy wasn't going to run anywhere – velcro-like was Figaro's mode of adherence. Figaro greeted Leppy with a warmth that never waned. With a perseverance that bespoke a life-long love, as if of one made long before his birth. On Leppy's part though, the first flush of "How-de-do" quickly faded.

Over the next several weeks, the words most appropriate to describe Leppy's demeanor towards the newcomer were: reticent; standoffish; apprehensive; and wary. The puppy for his part loved to punk Leppy's muzzle with his front paws as he stood on tippy toes of his back legs. Figaro – at any quiet moment when Leppy was laying down and at puppy eye-level – would grab onto Leporello's silk-purse ears and chew, chew, chew. Also, Figaro sought comfy contact with him whenever Leppy was recumbent. Figaro would contort himself to fit between Leppy's front legs, or Leppy's back legs, or curl up in the warmth of his belly area. Leppy seemed to resent this behavior more than any other. Since Sunny doted on the puppy with shameless abandon, at annoyed times Leporello would turn his Mary-Pickford-eyes to him and ask "When is this one going home?" Later, the pleading changed to "Won't you let me put him in his place?" Around this same time, Sunny wanted a portrait. He sat with Leppy on his right and squiggle-bottom on his left. I, behind the camera, captured a series of shots – first Leppy leaning away with all his might and casting a suspicious glare at the 'thing' on Sunny's other side. Then a second shot of puppy leaping across Sunny's lap. And a third with a sad and frank-looking Leppy casting his eyes right in the camera as Figaro sank his puppy teeth into a silk-purse ear.

But Figaro had time on his side, and his creamy, doe-eyed perseverance eventually worked its magic. The Airedale's grudging standoffishness grew to become shoulder-shrugging permittance, and eventually, deep-sighing acceptance. He played it cool and thought he never quite let on how he'd started looking forward to the seeping comfort Leporello derived from Figaro's close contact. They began to nap together, and Leppy commenced to look for him when the younger dog was absent from his side. I should relay the little bit of Leppy brand discipline he finally conveyed, though always with a deferential regard to Sunny's face. One evening, Sunny came home, and the two ran a joyful riot to greet him. Figaro though, far from wasting his attention on Sunny, usually focused on pushing Leppy's face with his paws, along with other annoying activities. Well, one evening, Leppy deftly whipped around and pinched the inside of one of Figaro's abundantly fleshed Cocker Spaniel ears. The puppy seemed shocked, squealed like a stuck pig, and left Leporello alone. Leppy glanced up to get Sunny's approval, and once obtained, this made him feel more at ease.

ह ह ह ह

Thoughts of Figaro's heart-break should Leppy go from the scene, plus knowledge of Leppy's superior parenting skills, led us to decide on opening our doors to another puppy. Masetto the Airedale came to us Thanksgiving week 2010. Born in the middle of July, he too was a good age for a new home and had grown up with his parents and siblings. The pushings of youth will always push, and as he latched onto Figaro, he became a link to that new green day. Masetto chewed Figaro's ears, he'd plop down where Figaro tried to walk and exposed his belly for Figaro's play. He would crowd Figaro for rest and generally did to him as he had done to Leporello. Masetto with Lep was different. This pup treated Leporello with the dignity due the head of the pack. Leppy would put his two cents in whenever he thought Masetto was too boisterous with Fig, and then the younger would listen and back off. The one supreme expression of affection from Airedale pup to Airedale senior was grooming. Masetto would lick Leppy's ears on the inside, and Leppy, despite all efforts at suppression, would positively reel with the pleasure. He'd groan low and crane his ear canal closer to the puppy's cleaning touch. Masetto would also take care of Leppy's tired eyes. Though they could not see as well as they had, they benefited from direct stimulation and careful clearing of gunk. Masetto would do this in gentle repetitiveness – over and over his soothing licks would pass over Leppy's shut eyes. Gentle piled upon gentle, the slow rhythm would make Masetto close his eyes too.

A couple of months before his passing, Leppy completely blew his Cool-Hand-Luke persona regarding Figaro. One day I was typing at the computer, as I am now, and I was vaguely aware that Leppy was lying on the floor in the room adjacent. Had I glanced, I'm sure I would have seen his face through the open door. Concentrating on my work, Figaro appeared at my feet, hotly chased by Masetto in play. They tussled for a few minutes between my legs until I grudgingly picked Figaro up and put him on my lap. I worked away and ten minutes later set Figaro down. Masetto began to roughhouse again, and about thirty seconds later, as if out of nowhere, Leppy was a lightning rush of protection over Figaro. He was angry. Hard for me to believe, but angry is the only word that describes the way he chastised puppy. "Leave him alone," he insisted, for Leppy had had enough. The puppy did so and retreated to a faraway room. Figaro's perseverance had won over his big Airedale heart after all.

Perseverance, always optimistic, always green, pushes on luxury and wins. Many times, as in the case of the kinder-garten child, aged sternness affects youth's development for the better, and steady growth reminds budding mortality where it has sprung from. I saw Masetto only last evening cleaning Figaro's eyes. Figaro lay on the sofa, his head positioned forward where Masetto, standing on the floor, could groom for a long, steady time. Masetto after a moment or two rolled his eyes back and continued with his eyes tightly shut. Why? Pleasure. Like the flush of a first kiss, long-lasting devotion too has a pervasive sweetness that overwhelms the other senses until they shut down in the absolute reception of love. Max did so with his parakeet; Leppy with Masetto. The push to pleasure through connection is a constant on all of us, if only we obey its insis-tence with open-hearted relish.

ESSAY VII:
Masetto and the Tennis Ball

We are told that God created man in his own image. We are then told how man quickly revealed shortcomings. God's disappointment, for those who hold the faith, is an ongoing limitation on our potential – our ability to connect with the flawless within ourselves. Of all of God's manifest creations, man is his least honest, with himself, with the face he shows to others, and with his inherent potential to godliness. Of all of man's many petty creations, working with what scraps we found around us, Dog is our greatest. For in him we stamped not our own image in flawed coinage, but we created an honest portrayal of divine selflessness, and crowned him with the polar reward of man's infidelity. Dog is man's best creation, because we made him in God's image. There is a Zen conundrum, of the "if a tree falls in the woods . . . " ilk. The puzzle I am thinking of goes like this: Lord Buddha said a dog is free from the wheel of Dharma (the cycle of birth and rebirth), but a later master instructed that a dog can never be taught to be enlightened. How can that be? Now, the reason these conundrums exist is not to generate answers, not to even generate thoughts towards an answer, but to release thought from its own wheel of pointless roundabout misery. The goal of these puzzles is to free a seeking mind from its restless disease of philosophy – there is no answer. But my mind, afflicted as it still is with thought, thinks the dog puzzle is an easy one. Dogs are born enlightened. They suffer none of the limiting ambition and scheming avarice that seems to be man's self-appointed birthmark. To instruct them on godliness would be to presume to instruct God on the ecstasies of Dogliness.

Chip Brown, in his 1990 article on Airedales, mentions visiting with a family of these dogs. They offered their tennis balls to him as he sat – in the same fashion as Max had done to me – a test, they would not let go. Masetto, now eight months old, does this same Airedale thing. He grips the ball, holds it to my hand and then eyes me while he tenaciously grips it against my pulling. An eternal push; spring to spring to spring.

Tennis balls remind me of the many cutting room floor items that will not be elaborated on today. Like, how Leppy barked at a police horse and earned himself (that is, earned me) a ticket; how he would pull me into the open door of every hair salon or barber shop expecting to find a stadium full of people there (each hair on the floor speaking of an individual's presence); how a mean old Scottie, unprovoked, bit him on the top of his nose and produced a scar there until his dying days; how he survived, one of the first dogs anywhere to do so, his bout with deadly melanoma via a new cancer vaccine; how he relished the flavor of carrots and of a particular soft-leaf weed that grows round about here; or how he would barge into the neighbor's upstairs place to chase her wonderful cat Toro. Leppy, a bungling Keystone Kop of a lout, was never any match for fleet-sensed Toro.

But balls – tennis balls, with their bounce – were his favorite toys. Social instruments as well as fun, he derived much from them. We could give a thousand, straight-from-the-package examples, but the gutter balls he found on the street: these he'd hold onto all the way back home, sometimes the tongue lolling from the side of his mouth, the heat no match for the joy the foundling ball provided. A veritable conundrum-sized problem arose when he chanced to find two gutter balls on the same outing. One would be dropped, the other picked up; dropped, again; picked up, etc., etc. Finally, he'd look to me, and I'd have to carry one of these grotty balls for its proud new owner. At the peak of youthful vigor we would take him to the double tennis courts at Corona Heights, and with the battered badminton racket Sunny picked out of the trash one day, hit ball after ball to him. He'd run into position, catch the ball in his mouth, drop it, and catch the next hit to him. After we exhausted our bagful of balls, we'd move to the other side of the court; I'd collect the balls, and Sunny would hit them back to Leppy waiting on the other side of the net. He could go on for an hour under the cloudless blue sky without even a pause, so we'd have to roll the balls into the far corners of the court and make him chase them one by one. Twenty minutes of this, and he'd finally plop down for a rest. A brief three minute respite, with sloppy tongue to the breeze, and he'd be up again ready to repeat the whole exercise. He loved the courts even when we were not on them, because I'd take him through the gates and to the trash cans. Pulling off the lid, Leppy would jump with front paws on the rim, and watch me extract discarded balls. Usually there'd be enough to fill a bag and one left over for his mouth to grip all the way home. How happy was he!

In the park he'd exhibit his social skills with tennis balls. He was never possessive, never broke his calm self-possession just because some dog 'stole' his ball. If he chased one we threw for him, and his trudge was interrupted on the way back by the chance meeting of another dog, the ball would be forgotten. Dropped in the grass, another dog to play with was always preferred. If that same dog, usually wary-eyed, bent down to pick up Leppy's ball, he would positively present the body language of "Take it. It's yours!"

🍒   🍒   🍒   🍒

Masetto doesn't have the same energy level. He plays a few minutes with a ball and seems to be fully satisfied. When Masetto's age, Leporello would wake up in the middle of the night and play quietly for an hour or so in the dark. He'd toss the ball for himself, then scamper down our long hallway after it. He'd do this repeatedly, never bothering us, until he felt relaxed again. He never was a settled sleeper either. He pre-ferred to get up and change position at least once an hour. Masetto in complete contrast, plonks down and snoozes the night away in one cozy spot.

Dogs look to us for the same guidance as we look to God. How ironic that while we look to a superior force of purity and love, they are forced to love an inferior example than them-selves. It started on Labor Day 2010, the day that Leppy's mortality was wedged into my immediate perspective. We visited friends in Bodega Bay. They insisted we bring Leppy and Figgy, but had they mentioned anything about their cats, we would not have brought them. Walking into their home, Leppy bumped into a feline who was napping. A quick swipe of the claw opened a tiny cut on Leppy's right lower eyelid. A virus had been introduced to his system, but my only thought at the time was "we dodged a bullet with that one," because his eye had not been scratched. A clean up of the trickle of blood, a dab of hydrogen peroxide and all seemed well. A check of the wound in the next couple of days shows a complete external healing, so the event was all but forgotten. So forgotten, that in the second week of October, when Doctor Fong told me Leporello was near death, and he asked me seemingly nonsense questions about where Leppy had been, I could not come up with the cat scratch. He asked me, could Leppy have encountered a raccoon? Was he digging and ingesting garden dirt? A virus, he said, one present in the natural environment could be causing Leppy's renal failure. No, I said, no raccoons, no dirt – it was more than a month later that I recalled the scratch from an outdoor cat's claw and the day of transmission.

☙ ☙ ☙ ☙

At the beginning of October, he went in for a regular checkup and everything seemed fine. Airedales have a notorious tolerance for pain, and when young, the only true way to know they feel under the weather is to gauge their badness. If they suddenly become angels, take them to the vet; something's wrong. At Leppy's age, he was a continual angel, so that standard no longer applied. I mentioned to the doctor his slowing down, but nothing suggested that a blood test was needed. After that, Leppy slowly became ill. No fever, no loss of appetite, but his drinking increased, his energy continued to decrease, and finally, ever loosening stools appeared. If a fever had appeared I would have known to take him back to the vet sooner, but by the second week of October, his prognosis was very grim. The morning I took him in again he had vomited, he had stopped eating, and he had full-blown diarrhea. The doctor told me they'd start fluids and intravenous antibiotics. Broached next was the subject of euthanasia. I respect each difficult decision ever made in this regard, but somehow I always 'knew' two things about Leporello: one, he'd live to be fifteen; and two, he'd pass at home with Sunny and me by his side. These were things I never consciously thought about, or had as goals, they were just always there, in the back of my mind, obtained at time unknown or by channel unexplained. But, there I was, my fourteen-year-old dog on the verge of being humanely killed before a virus murdered him in the hospital. "Do what you can," I said. He was no better, in fact much worse, 9 hours later when

I picked him up from his regular vet. They had no overnight care, so decision number two had to be made. Take him home, home to die that night, or take him to the referral doctors with their 24/7 treatment facilities. We picked up the tired-looking but still ambulatory Leppy and took him to the overnight care facility. They continued his treatment of fluids and antibiotics. At 6 AM he was to receive another blood test with immediate processing. If his blood toxicity was not on the rebound, another decision would have to be made. The phone rang at 7 o'clock – not only no better, but worse. Forgetting her impeccable bedside manner, the doctor wondered out loud how it was that Leppy was still conscious with the reported levels of coma-inducing poison in his blood. I told her, he's coming home – no more needles; no more fluorescent lighting; just peace.

I have to say I was shocked to see Leppy twenty minutes later. He was barely able to walk that morning as he came through the ward doors to me in the waiting room. The overnight nurse who had cared for him the entire time slowly led a dog who acted so out of sorts, he did not immediately react to my presence. I was handed his lead and told the doctor wanted to talk to me, but my thought was to get Lep into the car. As I hoisted him into the back of our SUV and settled him on a blanket, he looked up at me. Those same guileless eyes that have looked at me for all those years from the picture frame – from that first Sunday we had him – they looked straight into me. "So tired," they said. "I'm so tired – you understand me."

The doctor came rushing out to the car. She looked like she was about to cry. "I'm so sorry," she told me. "I'm so sorry."

"No," I said, glancing through the open car door. Leppy had repositioned himself to face the two of us. "No. Please call his vet and tell them we'll try one more day of treatment. One more day."

Something passed in that look. The 'something' to me was clear, but I must have conveyed another thing to Leporello, something that let him know I was supremely unready to lose him, and he, though he probably wanted to continue on to comforting rest, decided selflessly to fight. He, I firmly believe, at that moment fought on for my sake. In the very ecstasy of his own supreme suffering, he thought first of my pain, and my suffering was something he could not abide. He grasped onto love with the same tenacity as on a tennis ball. He would not let go, if I could not let go.

At the end of another nine hours, I took him home, but I could tell a marked improvement had occurred. The near-zombie of the morning was gone. He greeted me with tired jubilation and anxious energy to go home. The staff reported good news – he had eaten. The caregiver dedicated to assisting him that day had been inspired to try baby food: puréed turkey. Patiently he enticed an at-first-apathetic Leporello. He then rubbed some on his patient's gums, and Leppy, despite himself, developed an appetite. Reluctantly at first, then with relish, he polished off several jars. This same nurse instructed me on how to give the fluids at home, Doctor Fong saying there was a chance his kidneys would be kick-started back into some function. This, with antibiotics, was Leppy's only chance, but at dark-horse odds.

Getting Leppy settled at home, he showed no interest in the rugs, or carpet, but was actively sniffing for Figaro. Once he assured himself his little Cocker charge was safe and secure, Leppy settled down on his couch in the kitchen with obvious relief. Figaro, never one to stand on ceremony, sidled up to Leppy's flank and curled up in his belly section. Leppy for his part, as far as anyone could observe by his cool demeanor, positively curled up around the Cocker Spaniel in comfortable reciprocation. He was home.

🍒 🍒 🍒 🍒

The super volume of fluids introduced into his system meant he had to go outside every 3 hours. I'd help him stand, but otherwise he'd take himself up the three broad steps to the garden from the back door and relieve himself. I prepared his food – chicken cooked with macaroni – and pulled out the baby food I bought before I picked him up. I tried rubbing it on the inside of his gum, but he didn't seem too interested. I prayed the next morning would find him hungry. To be ready to assist him during the night, I moved the outdoor sofa cushion indoors and arranged it on the kitchen floor next to Leppy's couch. We slept that way – he sleeping more than I did – shaking off all those needles and fluorescent lights in a dark dreamless sleep. In the morning, I retried the baby food, and he seemed just as unin-terested. This more than anything panicked me. He motivated running on several days with very little nourishment, and he could die from lack of strength. Something inspired me to try another way. A new approach – I dabbed some on the top of his nose. Out of sheer annoyance, his tongue would make an appearance and wipe it clean. After ten or so licks, I suppose the saliva glands were stimulated and the flavor in his mouth created an appetite. Soon he was licking it off my finger, then out of the jar, then another jar, then another. By afternoon, he was gingerly picking chicken pieces out of the macaroni. Then by evening, he was eating the starch too. But back in the morning, after he had something in his stomach, I gave him a liter of fluids and he napped soundly with Figaro at his side. Repeating this, my sleeping in the kitchen, staying up late watching late 1980s *Friday the 13th: the Series* reruns on TV and trying to get myself tired enough to go to sleep for three hours, Leppy and I passed many nights to come. But within a couple of days of our new routine, unbelievably – unbelievable for anyone who does not know what an Airedale who's made up his mind can do – he improved. He began to eat his full. His stool returned to normal, and by the second week, he was wagging his tail at the sight of Doctor Fong.

"Have you met the Lazarus dog!" I called out to the vet from the waiting room.

Hard to believe, but by Halloween, not only was he better, but he was better than in the weeks before his illness. His fluid volume was reduced to a third, to 500 milliliters daily, and his body adjusted to his new situation with complete continence. I stopped sleeping in the kitchen, and Leppy too returned to the bedroom and his bed. Upstairs was warmer, and cozier with all four of us resuming our slumber routine.

But like the character of Mary in *Little Women*, the recovery may have been full, but the constitution was weakened. Like Mary's, Leppy's time was limited. Miracle it felt on November 4th, 2010, to celebrate his fifteenth birthday. He tore open his presents with the same gusto as he did on his first. These days – six months and one day extra to be exact – were not selfish days. He resumed doing what was routine, walking the familiar sidewalks, and touching people like the open-armed baby in the stroller, and our lady neighbor into whose hugs he settled to receive her gentle "I love you."

There were ups and downs, but Thanksgiving was a time for all his human friends to visit with him. He relished their attention, and his new charge, Masetto, learned by example how an Airedale properly attends a court of admirers. By Christmas, there was more wrapping paper to rip open, though he left all the toy contents to Masetto and Figaro to play with. Each morning I spent a couple of hours on his medical care, but these tasks were never very demanding. These few days since he died, I have kept this time – the time I spent on him – to write these essays. These hours set aside for him are not easy for me to give up, but with the time used to try and heal him, I have turned the proverbial clock, and borrowed his minutes no longer needed to try and heal myself.

When Leppy died, the layers of my grief seemed to focus on a certain bleakness of perspective. Namely, for fifteen years – looking backwards – I could find his presence there in each and every day. But looking forward, a future loomed where he did not exist in even one more of those days. But, by writing these seven essays, one every day for a week, I have cheated death, for at least in seven of these endlessly bleak days that stretch *ad nauseam* to my own death, Leporello walked with me. I forced him to be with me so that he will ever be here with me. I hope he chooses to remain through choice, but either way, I know I let him go – that I can let him go now, knowing that sooner or later, we will walk again together. I have less fear now that I shall forget his sweet alkaline scent, and I have better ascended faith's rungs that I shall smell Leppy's sweet presence again, when I am ready – when I am worthy.

ॐ ॐ ॐ ॐ

Yesterday we picked up his remains. They rode in my lap back home, the sad remainder of us taking that little pup from Max and Abby Gail's side, and of that trip when he first came home with us. Then a certain plain mouse toy awaited him, and now a certain emptiness awaited the rest of us. After his passing – peacefully on his couch with us gathered around – Sunny and I performed the rites of family. We observed his obsequies with tear-stained eyes, wiping him clean from head to tail with moist towelettes and laying him down on the blanket from our bed. This blanket Sunny bought in Japan specifically for Leppy's comfort and one that could be a bedspread against his nails that frayed all others. Sunny removed the name tag from his collar and placed it near his head, below his chin. When he was dying – the minute or two after he stopped breathing, but his heart continued to rush blood to his brain – I summoned all my strength and asked Max to come and lead him to them – to his mother and brothers and sisters, and I know he was there, there to collect his child from us as we had from him. Sunny placed the tag so Leppy could recognize his remains if he had to, and so that others could identify him too. For my part, I knew what I had to do, though it broke my heart. I went to retrieve a well-loved, faintly soiled little object. Without its blue-lined ears, or its rope tail, the mouse was otherwise intact. Leppy had ripped and eviscerated any number of toys of their stuffing – a hundred, perhaps – but through all the years he left his mouse alone. I placed it on the blanket with him – I did not want to – but I knew I had no right to keep it anymore. It went with him.

On the way home, I mentioned to Sunny that I had been thinking. Some of his ashes we should keep with us, but with the rest, we should set him free. Free to run amongst the dogs in the parks he loved: Corona Heights, Buena Vista, and especially in Duboce Park. We must share him with those he loved. And that's what we did.

I started this project with one question in mind: How can a Creator, a creator we are raised to believe exists in pure love, allow pain to exist? How can he in his creation have opened a door for loss to creep in? If he loved us, how can he have wrought in that love a pain that tempers love at the same moment? But, perhaps suffering is the one aspect of the Divine that we are allowed. Perhaps it is suffering that acts through the muddling confusion of human conceit itself. It tells us we are not the dashing, the urbane or polished, the artless, the self-possessed or meekly-lost people we fancy ourselves to be, sometimes in turns, sometimes all in a jumble. No, we are at best, faulty reflectors of the Divine moment when flashed the bitterest pain that God picked at the start of this world. For when a parent has to watch their child die before them of old age, we assume God's vantage – we are forced to see a plain stretch before us of lonely and seemingly helpless sorrow.

আ আ আ আ

When I was a child, and out riding with my father, for he loved his twilight rambles, I would ask him if he knew what God's favorite color was. "Green," I'd tell him myself, "just look around!" And so God's green ever pushes, always new, always at the pinnacle of optimism, and thus pushing, like Masetto closing his eyes to better take in the relishing of life and its emotions – the same as Max did with his parakeet. I too close my eyes, and I see Leporello. I close my eyes, and the force of ecstasy there I will tenaciously hold to myself. Through his image I will be able to remind myself, in dark days ahead, of the true force of Love, of God, and of Dog.

NOTES AND OTHER AIREDALE ITEMS OF INTEREST

The updatable nature of the internet means some material documented here may have been moved or deleted. If so, copy the name of the content and content-creator, and then search online. Alternates will most likely be easy to locate.

ACB

TEXT ENDNOTES

[1] "The Life and Opinions of Tristram Shandy, Gentleman" Laurence Sterne (London 1759). The first-person narrator is famous for starting his biography not with his birth, but with the moment his father and mother conceived him.

https://archive.org/details/lifeandopinions01un
kngoog/page/n10/mode/2up

[2] "The Dog That Bit People" James Thurber, reprinted in *The Thurber Carnival* (New York 1945), ps. 214-220

https://archive.org/details/thurbercarnival0000
unse/page/214/mode/2up

— And here's the beginning of Thurber's story showing the sketch he made of Muggs the Airedale:

https://i.pinimg.com/564x/25/71/fb/2571fb2866
7f1db54c1a5ca6c9874ccc.jpg

[3] "Style, Brains, and Clownish Wit: Everything One Looks for in a Spouse" Chip Brown, the January edition of *Connoisseur Magazine* (New York 1990), ps. 58-63

https://archive.org/details/connoisseurillus220j
anlon/page/n67/mode/2up

— Or, for a text-only version posted by Mr. Brown himself, see:

https://www.chipbrown.net/articles/style.htm

– And here's a standalone image of the magazine cover:

https://i.pinimg.com/564x/46/00/29/460029583
f77c175b23d8ea620b7a436.jpg

[4] "Walks with Leporello" joins what is arguably an over-represented literary genre involving any particular single type of dog, especially as this breed's popularity has shrunk considerably since its 1920s highwater mark. That being said, the remarkable traits of love and companionship offered in abundance by Airedales has ensured its literary canon of praise continues unaffected by any transient tastes in other canines. See the "Airedale in Popular Culture" section below for a partial list of literature for this type of terrier, both fiction and biographical.

[5] Only in June 2022, while I was preparing this text for the press, did I encounter a piece that may be considered a true predecessor of *Walks With Leporello*. Perhaps by way of happy accident, or by preordained destiny, I've recently been listening to episodes of Tallulah Bankhead's ninety-minute-long *The Big Show*, which was broadcast by NBC radio. *The Big Show* offered comedy and music, and somewhat more uniquely for primetime listening, dramatic scenes and readings. On the March 11th,

1951, program, Bankhead read from Oscar Odd McIntyre's 1923 *Cosmopolitan Magazine* essay "Missing Junior." The best-selling author had a syndicated daily column about life in New York City as an outsider, and can be best understood as a cross between O. Henry and Alistair Cooke. As the man's work is woefully under-represented on the internet, I've typed up a transcript of McIntyre's moving essay from the broadcast and posted it here:

https://gayauthors.org/stories/chapter/19666-vii-masetto-and-the-tennis-ball/?do=findComment&comment=529160

[6] In regards to the Teddy Roosevelt quote, see this 1925 "Doggiest Dog" affirmation of the President's opinion:

https://i.pinimg.com/564x/b1/fc/eb/b1fcebbe16a279c16ed5dc8706d6d395.jpg

— There is some disagreement concerning whether the verb spoken by the President was "lick" (as in defeat), or "whip." I tend to believe *lick* sounds more like TR, and its slightly antiquated associations by the 1920s may explain why whip was placed in the quote as a substitute.

[7] "Flipper" was a television series centered on the interactions of a wild Florida dolphin with two young brothers. Although its initial broadcast lasted from 1964 to 1967, it was in syndicated

rerun when I was a child, and one of my favorites at an early age.

[8] The Ford LTD was a very popular mid-market sedan at the time, known for its roomy comfort and powerful engine.

[9] "Thanksgiving Memories: Pumpkin Desserts and Turkey Pot-pies" Julia Child, the November edition of *Wine & Food Magazine* (New York 1997), ps. 171-172 (the second link includes a picture of Eric the Airedale)

https://www.pinterest.com/pin/8192329884806
22533

https://www.pinterest.com/pin/8192329884806
22490/

[10] See Robert Manning Palmer's *All About Airedales: A Book of General Information Valuable to Dog Lovers and Owners, Breeders and Fanciers, Illustrated from Select Photographs of Noted Dogs and Rare Scenes – The Airedale Terrier Reviewed* (Seattle 1911), 5th Edition, 1915, ps. 122-123

https://books.google.com/books?id=4RcPAAA
AYAAJ&printsec=frontcover&source=gbs_ge_
summary_r&cad=0#v=onepage&q&f=false

[11] The fact there were two Airedale victims of the Titanic dis-aster is not in dispute. Survivors report that it was none other than John Jacob Astor who went to the ship's kennel and released all the caged dogs so they'd have a fighting chance at survival. The man did so, according to his son's later report, because, while the boy and his mother were being loaded in a lifeboat, he pleaded with his father to look after the child's Airedale named "Kittie." Mr. Astor and Kittie both succumbed in the icy waters. The identity of the second First Class passenger Airedale is somewhat in doubt due to a lesser degree of documentation. According to the researcher below, part of the confusion lies in the dog's given name being "Airedale." See Patty Inglish's April 10th, 2019, article *What Happened to Pets and Other Animals on the Titanic in 1912?* posted on hubpages.com

https://discover.hubpages.com/animals/What-
Happened-To-the-Pets-and-Other-Animals-on-
the-Titanic-in-
1912#gid=ci0272eba2a00127da&pid=what-
happened-to-the-pets-and-other-animals-on-the-
titanic-in-1912-MTc2NDYyNDE4MzE3NDIwNTA2

[12] Photos of running cougars up trees in California, see Robert Manning Palmer *All About Airedales* (as detailed in Endnote No. 9), p. 104. Also see ps. 58 and 81 for more Airedale "lion hunting" in the American West.

https://books.google.com/books?id=4RcPAAA AYAAJ&printsec=frontcover&source=gbs_ge_ summary_r&cad=0#v=onepage&q&f=false

[13] Here is a California photo of an Airedale. Dating from the late 1850s or early 1860s, it is the very oldest known photographic representation of the breed, and shows a dog remarkably like the standard modern Airedales to be found in the Western United States today.

https://i.pinimg.com/564x/c4/96/ce/c496ce584 e0017a16b206dd265a4a18b.jpg

– And for those itching to "debunk" this image by dismissively trying to pass off the canine as an otterhound, I will point out the irrefutable. The dog in the picture has easily identifiable terrier qualities. For one, the nature of its coat stands out (which is wiry and nothing like the other hound's smooth, silky coat); two, it's flattened head is quite evident (as opposed to an otterhound's domed pate); and three, the relatively small ears are dead giveaways that this is an

Airedale (as extra-large, droopy ears are characteristic for otterhounds).

[14] 1905 photograph of President Teddy Roosevelt with his Airedale. It was first published by Niall Kelly in *Presidential Pets* (New York 1992), p. 50

https://i.pinimg.com/564x/3e/77/81/3e77813cc
7e45048d8cd0fcffdaa8463.jpg

— And here is TR hunting with his Airedale in the snow:

https://i.pinimg.com/564x/81/51/06/815106b8a
75873c7095b2ec2e3fa9b4e.jpg

[15] An illustration of President Woodrow Wilson's Airedale, Davie:

https://i.pinimg.com/564x/9d/f2/5e/9df25ed6b9
eb29582ca2e885fd92cf4c.jpg

– And here is Davie with Wilson X. Jackson in 1916, his groomer / handler / caregiver. Mr. Jackson began working at the White House as a messenger, but his special way Davie (and all Airedales it seems) made him indispensable as the trainer of several generations of presidential pets. You will see him in most of the casual photographs of Laddie Boy, who was especially close to Mr. Jackson. He also served under the Coolidge and Hoover administrations, taking care of their respective canines as well.

https://i.pinimg.com/564x/c6/94/b7/c694b7c3e
6b0e11ac6d7f972ab597202.jpg

[16] Calvin and Grace Coolidge had two White House Airedales. Here is the First Lady with either Paul Pry (brother of Laddie Boy), or Laddie Buck (son of Laddie Boy):

https://i.pinimg.com/564x/38/82/f8/3882f84e32
c3c50050fef5a7a825f85e.jpg

– And here is a Marine Colonel visitor to the White House holding Laddie Buck as a puppy:

https://i.pinimg.com/564x/d2/25/0e/d2250ebf4
331a4d9d294800c429e18d0.jpg

[17] When reading about the subject of presidential pets, Laddie Boy's special bond with the First Family, and in the hearts of Americans all across the world, will easily allow one to see why this Airedale is singled out for special mention. It never seems overstatement to suggest the simple fact that Laddie Boy was the most beloved dog to ever reside in the White House. If you need proof of such, then tell me which other chief executive companion had 20,000 American children donate their own personal money to build a permanent White House memorial to them? None, is the answer.

[18] The news photograph of Laddie Boy fretting as the President lay dying across the country now resides at the Library of Congress, and is in the public domain. You can find it here:

https://www.loc.gov/pictures/item/2016847782/

So acclaimed was Harding's companion and best friend, that I invite you to view the special section which follows. It is devoted to a remarkable Airedale's life and legacy.

LADDIE BOY'S OWN GALLERY

There is a charming account of six-month-old Laddie Boy arriving in the West Wing just as the Administration's first Cabinet meeting was underway. The President was so enamored with the Airedale gift, he walked out to immediately play with the puppy on the White House lawn. Accurate tale or not, the abounding love Laddie Boy had for Harding makes it certain the pair enjoyed early and intense bonding sessions. The collection that follows hints at just how special this connection of man and dog was.

» First, images of Laddie Boy, Florence and Warren Harding on the White House balcony, with an adorning crowd gathered on the lawn to greet them.

https://i.pinimg.com/564x/88/79/b5/8879b5ff6e
13e73b64f71e18e5120c15.jpg

https://i.pinimg.com/564x/7a/b9/53/7ab9538fb
8a0219aaa82e5829017e1ab.jpg

— A detail from the same photograph:

https://i.pinimg.com/564x/b8/b7/67/b8b76701c
0bc6ff1e608524911fe6ab3.jpg

» Laddie Boy garnered quite a lot of press coverage, becoming the original First Pet of his nation, with all the public following that it generated. However, here we see the humble beginnings; a small notice that a breeder had handed a puppy over to the President. It ran in the March 8th, 1921, *Birmingham News* (Alabama), and reads:

DOG GIVEN HARDING
Laddy Boy Will Become Pet of the
White House.

WASHINGTON, March 5.—President Harding was presented today with an Airedale dog, Laddy Boy, who because of the fondness of the new chief executive for dogs is expected to become the most popular of the White House pets.

The presentation was made by Charles W. Quetsche of Toledo, Ohio, who said the father of Laddy Boy was "Tender and Tiptop," champion Airedale of the United States.

https://i.pinimg.com/564x/cd/30/36/cd3036b33
b556b6abf79635516313c4b.jpg

– From the June 13th, 1923, *Washington Evening Star,* we can see Laddie Boy was issued the first tax-paid dog tag in the District.

https://i.pinimg.com/564x/a0/ac/3f/a0ac3f5e17
e707a4e76890dd6cac0810.jpg

– From the January 7th, 1922, issue of the San Bernadino *Sun* newspaper, we get a candid glimpse of the Hardings at mealtime:

A Dog's Life.

Laddie Boy begs for surreptitious helpings and gobbles your fingers just like your own pet dog does at home. Across the table, the only person who can address the President with perfect impunity says, "Warren, leave that dog alone. Laddie, come here."

https://i.pinimg.com/564x/51/c2/57/51c257105
37f73663ad2a7e7530fc072.jpg

– The press coverage generated this December 16th, 1922, letter from a pair of little girls in New York City. It reads almost as an approximation to a letter for Santa Claus.

Dear Mr. President,

We have seen your Doggy's picture in the Newspaper. We think he is an awfully nice Boy. Eleanor Kingsbury was at our school and she showed us the picture of you which you had sent her. At school we had an election for president [and] you had much more than Mr. Cox.

It must be fun living in that great big white–house! Don't you think its nice Christmas is so near! We do! We are both going to get dolls from Santa! At least, if we are good.

We hope you and your Airedale Doggy have a Merry Christmas!

      With love,
        Betsy Clark
        Katharine Jones

https://i.pinimg.com/564x/55/a9/48/55a948dbc3b21e4dc8695fdb09cd0e1b.jpg

— The President replied!

December 18, 1922.

Dear Betsy and Katharine:

Thank you both very much for your note. I wish you could both see Laddie Boy in real life instead of in the newspapers. He is just as good a dog lying in front of me in my study in the evening as he is in the newspapers.

I hope the both of you will have a very happy Christmas, and that meantime, you will be so persistently good that you will get the dolls you want Santa Claus to bring you.

From your friend,
[Warren Harding]

https://i.pinimg.com/564x/d9/af/97/d9af972703
dafa47835b5a478e19b1d3.jpg

» The newspaper-related items above were all documented by Marty Rhodes Figley in his February 10th, 2021, blog article *Laddie Boy, the 1st First Dog*. You can find it here:

http://martyrhodesfigley.blogspot.com/2021/02
/laddie-boy-1st-first-dog.html

— There are a few other serious studies of Laddie Boy online, like Diane Tedeschi's January 22, 2009, *Smithsonian Magazine* article *The White House's First Celebrity Dog,* posted here:

https://www.smithsonianmag.com/history/the-
white-houses-first-celebrity-dog-48373830/

— Doug Capra penned a six-part series for *The Seward Journal,* which initially began posting on October 14, 2020. The opening entry of *Laddie Boy, and President Warren G. Harding's 1923 Visit to Alaska* can be found here:

https://www.sewardjournal.com/features/sewar
ds_history/laddie-boy-and-president-warren-g-

harding-s-1923-visit-to-alaska-part-1/article_9c9f1b78-1498-11eb-933e-67b8456db74d.html#tncms-source=article-nav-next

– Margaret Truman, the once-famous singing daughter of the President, features the Airedale in her "Laddie Boy and Mr. Harding," which forms chapter 4 of her *White House Pets* (New York 1969), ps. 44-53:

https://archive.org/details/whitehousepets00trum/page/44/mode/2up

– Truman also discusses him in chapter 8, "The Calvin Coolidge Collection," ps. 86-104

https://archive.org/details/whitehousepets00trum/page/86/mode/2up

– "Our debut episode brings you the story of a good boy. A very good boy. Laddie Boy, the First Dog of the United States. A wonderful, charming terrier whom Americans loved[.]" So begins Duncan Fyfe and Alex Ashby's March 28, 2017, podcast entitled "The President's Dog." The full transcript is avail-able on their site *Idle Thumbs,* here:

https://www.idlethumbs.net/somethingtrue/epis
odes/the-presidents-dog

– Also, lastly, I'd recommend Louise Jones' more anec-
dotal "My Pet, the Airedale Terrier," which tells the story
of the Nation's beloved First Dog. It is posted in October
15, 2021 edition of *The Mountain Lines,* the news-letter of
the Retired Public Employees' Association of California,
ps. 7-9, available here:

https://www.rpea.com/view/download.php/cha
pter/078-oct21

» Laddie Boy greeted the President when he returned to the
White House with typical Airedale zeal. In the case of Harding's
pet, the press was always there to photograph and print Warren's welcome-homes. Here is a small selection of such images:

https://i.pinimg.com/564x/84/82/93/8482934b6
0a2e2e3812803baeecf2462.jpg

https://i.pinimg.com/564x/f7/6a/e7/f76ae7d899
3b46f5d30ae8577b051182.jpg

https://i.pinimg.com/564x/f8/ad/f7/f8adf73a33f
2750379a26e8df23742c4.jpg

https://i.pinimg.com/564x/dc/c8/14/dcc814a8df
acc2c51f58800e81447a06.jpg

https://i.pinimg.com/564x/d7/28/d6/d728d60c2
2be023c552fb8d533286534.jpg

https://i.pinimg.com/564x/6b/a2/84/6ba2845c7
ec2fd5ba6912d1a3cb91036.jpg

https://i.pinimg.com/564x/b3/ea/9d/b3ea9d7d1
079ff2c79bc46787ad8a198.jpg

» As First Pet of the Nation, portraits had to be procured of him for the official records. Laddie Boy made a fine subject, as these images will show.

— First, one with the canine and First Lady on the White House balcony. Florence Harding is wearing her official Girl Scouts of America uniform.

https://images.fineartamerica.com/images/artworkimages/mediumlarge/2/first-lady-florence-harding-in-girl-bettmann.jpg

– Here is another of the First Lady demonstrating the "shake" command she'd personally taught Laddie Boy.

https://i.pinimg.com/564x/7b/47/a9/7b47a913eb3bcad9dc769a8ca5e6d716.jpg

– And here is one on the White House Lawn with the President.

https://i.pinimg.com/564x/42/3b/41/423b41a8f44ce78e5bbce5689804e56c.jpg

– The Radiotine Process Company was all too happy to execute the pet's official White House portrait, to be hung on permanent display along with all the other official

First Family likenesses in the executive mansion. Here, Laddie Boy receives it on his third birthday:

https://i.pinimg.com/564x/77/8d/95/778d955d6
ec8195e0097377fbabf1bc3.jpg

https://i.pinimg.com/564x/e0/87/89/e087897e8
40ea266e273ecdbbaac7ecd.jpg

» Tributes poured in. Here is a charming homage via Margaret Shanks' 1921 poem, "The White House Joy"

Laddie Boy

You've a name that's leal an' true,
  Laddie Boy.
And your master's fond of you,
  Laddie Boy.
For a dog will stand the test
Of true friendship, give the best
To a state of life that's blest,
  Laddie Boy.

Brighten all your master's days,
    Laddie Boy.
Wag your tail when golf he plays,
    Laddie Boy.
Pressing hard from every road,
Be a mascot! – shift the load,
    Laddie Boy.

You will never understand,
    Laddie Boy.
That these lines to you were penned,
    Laddie Boy.
'Twas your name that caught my view,
Bonnie Scotland spoke through you,
Saying – write a screed or two
    To Laddie Boy.

https://i.pinimg.com/564x/05/1c/94/051c94266
611d712c25bd55bb056503a.jpg

– This six-and-a-half-inch statuette, finished in burnished gold, was offered for sale in and around many American cities. Laddie Boy is shown fetching the President's morning newspaper.

https://i.pinimg.com/564x/fd/d2/f0/fdd2f042883
380dee7e273e855ebcbc3.jpg

— For his third birthday, Laddie Boy received a multi-tiered birthday cake (made from dog biscuits) from Charles W. Quetsche, his Ohio breeder. The Airedale and the other canines of the White House enjoyed it, I'm sure.

https://i.pinimg.com/564x/77/a4/b8/77a4b8544
dadc635c81e5262c9126b12.jpg

https://i.pinimg.com/564x/30/f8/f5/30f8f560fb9f
93d709d0a988171179b6.jpg

https://i.pinimg.com/564x/ef/c4/a6/efc4a6ec5b
4db2b269768587e75c028b.jpg

» I will mention most of these images come from my personal gathering of them on Pinterest. These and many more of Laddie Boy may be found here:

https://www.pinterest.com/jojitown/laddie-boy/

» Bashka Paeff, the Boston sculptor who had earlier created the popular souvenir-size statuette of Laddie Boy, was chosen to render the life-size bronze memorial of the Airedale to be placed in the White House. The dog was fond of her, and traveled to her studio some twenty times while she crafted the clay maquette. Here she is in her work space with the First Pet of the nation and the completed model.

https://i.pinimg.com/564x/39/9a/4d/399a4d1d5
ab5d5e25ab0194c4181cc79.jpg

– Here is a photograph of the finished bronze on display in the Smithsonian.

https://i.pinimg.com/564x/86/23/d8/8623d865d
acf421d73673c898205495b.jpg

– A company in Ohio, the Hardings' home state, erected a memorial to Laddie Boy in the form of a beautifully radient stained-glass window. Note the stone-like curved elements around the Airedale's face. These are represent-tations of the Hardings' marble mausoleum.

https://i.pinimg.com/564x/67/86/e7/6786e742e
d3e6ac6233554b44d8e4bbc.jpg

https://i.pinimg.com/564x/67/a6/50/67a650359
ee6d2df123fdc89c2bb9987.jpg

» In regards to Laddie Boy's role of safeguarding the president, it's long past due that his statue be returned for visitors and admirers to pet at the White House. I say we start an online campaign to assure it happens. No one deserves it more than this most beloved of National pets.

THE AIREDALE IN POPULAR CULTURE

Gladys Brown Edwards says: "The Airedale is not a snobbish, aloof royalist. He is a product of modern times, with their handyman trends; hence he is not only Terrier Rex but is also the Royal Huntsman, the Palace Guard, and the Court Jester . . . he has an ebullient joy of life, yet has the calm dignity befitting his majesty."

» These attributes, plus their God-like ability to love, has made the breed especially popular figures in literature. Here is a representative list of books with Airedale heroes, although it's one that's far from complete.

— Clarence Budington Kelland' *Into His Own: The Story of an Airedale* (Philadelphia 1915)

https://i.pinimg.com/564x/1c/82/ed/1c82edd6d4efc0678bbccafc18f8d69d.jpg

— Eleanor Youmans' *Skitter Cat and Major* (Indianapolis 1925)

https://i.pinimg.com/564x/dd/78/4d/dd784d9e4
955c3cd4791388e289145df.jpg

— Vic Beamish's *Miss Perfection: The Illustrated Story of
an Airedale Terrier* (London 1931)

https://i.pinimg.com/564x/c2/14/7e/c2147e55a
84fe642614de60c856898de.jpg

— Guus Kuijer's *Olle: Met tekeningen van Thé Tjong-Khing*
("Olle: With illustrations by Thé Tjong-Khing") (Amsterdam 1990)

https://i.pinimg.com/564x/c8/c9/dd/c8c9ddb94
949235e219fe7acbfcb07e6.jpg

— Alexandra C. Jenkins' *Pal: the Story of an Airedale* (New
York 1930)

https://i.pinimg.com/564x/51/49/84/514984d21
8a8da780e1f702f9d6f3ba5.jpg

– Elizabeth Depp Hubbard Andrew Richards' *Person's Best Friend* (Richmond, Virginia [?] 1980)

https://i.pinimg.com/564x/4e/a1/d5/4ea1d5d26
f106374b57c1f2c0c985a86.jpg

– Horace Lytle's *The Story of Jack: A Tale of the North, and Other Fascinating Dog Stories* (Dayton 1920)

https://i.pinimg.com/564x/39/e3/b5/39e3b54f2
67818660ae5c8fcb782b13f.jpg

– Eleanor E. Helme / Nance Paul's *The Joker and Jerry Again* (London 1932)

https://i.pinimg.com/564x/41/91/61/41916182f
349d800e202e8a31dc81a9c.jpg

— Roselma Elliott's *Translated German Airedale – Terrier Articles No. 1* (New York [?] 1984)

https://i.pinimg.com/564x/8c/78/95/8c7895906
d855c662053646e34d99974.jpg

— Clarence Hawkes' *A Gentleman from France: an Airedale Hero* (Boston 1924)

https://i.pinimg.com/564x/33/84/98/338498df4
c9442e2178526519b265c32.jpg

— P. J. Ericson's *Diary of an Airedale* (New York 2015)

https://i.pinimg.com/564x/fa/7e/b8/fa7eb87f28
ca91569343a73eb197f12e.jpg

– Marjorie Flack's *Angus and Wag-Tail-Bess* (London 1930)

https://i.pinimg.com/564x/d1/e4/da/d1e4da2bc
6f4b1b287a2427ee96c9aa2.jpg

– D. A. Leonard *Karlo Dog: an Airedale* (Browarth Books 1989)

https://i.pinimg.com/564x/8e/52/93/8e5293429
e7fd7fcee10c5aa5439b292.jpg

– Dianne Haworth's *Paddy the Wanderer: the True Story of a Dog Who Captured the Heart of a City* (New York 2008)

https://i.pinimg.com/564x/79/44/0d/79440d22b
6a4b2e856a1c09d27b0a993.jpg

— Bill Molyneux / Sue Forrester's Emma's *Journey: Spirits of the High Country* (Toorak, VIC, Australia 2001)

https://i.pinimg.com/564x/0f/4c/61/0f4c61a47b
eb54e65efcad6814ec57c2.jpg

— Robin Reynolds' *Life to the Max: Maxims for a Great Life by a Dog named Max* (Tempe 2007)

https://books.google.com/books?id=hd_6QJPy
bRMC&printsec=frontcover&source=gbs_ge_s
ummary_r&cad=0#v=onepage&q&f=false

— Cecil Aldin's *Jack and Jill* (London 1914)

https://i.pinimg.com/564x/05/90/5f/05905fc2d9
efe4b0821f9e7ce1d1076f.jpg

– Fred M. Seale *Bogio* (Amarillo 1951)

https://i.pinimg.com/564x/c8/04/dd/c804dd3f89
401f77e8938104f028e577.jpg

– Peggy Iris Thomas' *A Ride in the Sun, or Gasoline Gypsy: A Dog is a Girl's Best Friend* (New York 1954)

https://i.pinimg.com/564x/b1/28/30/b12830cad
c630ea156f72388591811a4.jpg

– Horace Lytle's *Sandy: The Story of an Airedale* (New York 1926)

https://i.pinimg.com/564x/5d/a5/57/5da557b92
d50a849cfdd0562b8a0985f.jpg

– Samuel Davenport's *"YEL" – The Memories of a Happy Dog: The Point of View of Yel, Who Spent Most of His Life in the Royal Navy* (London 1924)

https://pethistories.wordpress.com/2017/08/17
/yel-the-memories-of-a-happy-dog/

– Elaine Hamilton's *I'm a Lucky Dog: by Jill, the Airedale* (London 1936)

https://i.pinimg.com/564x/9e/9c/2e/9e9c2ea83
e6a13066213a1a9830a68a6.jpg

– Paula Moekel's *Mein Hund Rolf: ein Rechnender und Buch-Strabierender Airedale Terrier* ["My Dog Rolf: an Airedale Terrier Summary and Primer"] (Stuttgart 1917)

https://i.pinimg.com/564x/6b/53/6d/6b536d304
877aa0ce26951570b3d4658.jpg

— Sylvestre C. Watkins' *Jeeps, a Dog for Defense* (Chicago 1944)

https://i.pinimg.com/564x/88/d0/fc/88d0fcca22
44ec6f78b10de4ab26f95f.jpg

» These dogs have oftentimes been the heroes of the movies in which they appear.

— The 1996 live-action version of the *1001 Dalmatians* story features the rescue of the puppies by Kipper, the Airedale. Here you can see his movie fan page:

https://101dalmatians.fandom.com/wiki/Kipper

— An earlier Disney live-action film from 1964 stars Jokyl Bengal II as an Airedale stranded on a voyage on the wrong ship, although a happy reunion is guaranteed in the end. *The Ballad of Hector the Stowaway Dog* was also released to theaters as "The Million Dollar Collar." You can listen to the movie's theme song here:

https://youtu.be/KSCk2IJUaUU

— The Airedale page on the movie-fan website "Reel Dogs" currently mentions the breed's appearance in 24 major films. This is by no means the total sum, and new movies are added by fans regularly. See here:

https://www.reeldogs.com/airedale/

» In addition to books and films, some fine artists have turned to this breed with a love and passion to capture their unique spirit.

— Ceramicist Nan Hamilton has painted them over and over again in true-to-life verve, clearly illustrating the joys of life with Airedales. See the following for a re-presentative sample of her art.

https://www.nanhamilton.com/gallery/dogwing
99/dogwing99.html

– Painter Lee Call has a special way of capturing the elusive glint in an Airedale's eyes, which is a patented blend of innocent intelligence and cunning scheming. See a sample of her work here:

https://i.pinimg.com/564x/b0/9a/0f/b09a0f727c
e45aebfaa90126e8f4c13b.jpg

https://images.fineartamerica.com/images/ar
tworkimages/mediumlarge/1/airedale-terrier-
apple-green-alicia-vannoy-call.jpg

– Illustrators have turned to Airedales time after time. The great versatility of their character makes them ideal for battle scenes, hunting forays, living room romps, or strolling down Fifth Avenue with the all swells. We will look at a few of these categories, starting first with how action-adventure magazines used them as their go-tos whenever bravery and heroism needed displaying on covers to sell issues. Here a small-but-representative sampling:

https://i.pinimg.com/564x/a1/79/89/a179894eb
d7d395af21169e395230b58.jpg

https://i.pinimg.com/564x/b6/a4/3f/b6a43fd5b8
164f58b5e5f6616cb9cf1d.jpg

https://i.pinimg.com/564x/dd/f3/7b/ddf37b121d
c7ca2540a08bb05f81cb71.jpg

https://i.pinimg.com/564x/87/5a/cb/875acbf6d7
9941ed575ee5180ec7f308.jpg

– Noble Airedales fighting for their countries:

https://i.pinimg.com/564x/58/df/15/58df159a8d
08a31c4328eee0f4a8a9b0.jpg

https://i.pinimg.com/564x/88/d0/fc/88d0fcca22
44ec6f78b10de4ab26f95f.jpg

https://i.pinimg.com/564x/4c/bc/75/4cbc75830
9d321988771b0ecb15804dd.jpg

https://i.pinimg.com/564x/0e/d8/ec/0ed8ecd64
56498ab2e09c168bbc58811.jpg

https://i.pinimg.com/564x/96/a8/38/96a838753
d15a2316c0aef4a12926945.jpg

https://i.pinimg.com/564x/4f/89/89/4f8989ea0d
acdf1a250dfa173e7b3666.jpg

– Glamor Dales on parade:

https://i.pinimg.com/564x/80/ac/f6/80acf61f7a5
c6e6d87c54b3976ae7b09.jpg

https://i.pinimg.com/564x/86/ba/10/86ba10901
3dfef375d2110451fa88b0c.jpg

https://i.pinimg.com/564x/54/f2/17/54f21732a9
2146e3dab81b897dadf80d.jpg

https://i.pinimg.com/564x/c4/c3/ac/c4c3ac11c0
f12dccde57f5d8d17cfb43.jpg

https://i.pinimg.com/564x/ce/15/9b/ce159b49c
689a14d1a8215624f85b842.jpg

https://i.pinimg.com/564x/1a/43/bf/1a43bfd322
0236dc508f9146c2d50341.jpg

— The breed shown in warm and cozy illustrations; i.e.,
Home is Where the Airedale is:

https://i.pinimg.com/564x/c8/82/6e/c8826ed71
0deca04d7ddb0bec80c0a78.jpg

https://i.pinimg.com/564x/7a/14/a3/7a14a3b80
b54e96d1bb14b1e0626824d.jpg

https://imgc.artprintimages.com/img/print/my-
guardian_u-l-
e68i20.jpg?artHeight=550&artPerspective=n&
artWidth=550&background=fbfbfb

https://i.pinimg.com/564x/cb/80/c2/cb80c28c3
129f5f7af742d591d2d79c1.jpg

— As Nature-loving adventure pups:

https://i.pinimg.com/564x/ba/b3/57/bab357737
f805b54932a1200c88654fe.jpg

https://i.pinimg.com/564x/7b/f2/1f/7bf21f2ae2d
273f904a9547fb4167f6c.jpg

https://i.pinimg.com/564x/01/a8/e5/01a8e5d6b
09862b111503bde32bb4d48.jpg

https://i.pinimg.com/564x/9d/7a/96/9d7a96fbe
9f0210a8630f3ffa08d195d.jpg

https://i.pinimg.com/564x/93/26/ce/9326ce6e3
2ccb8c950538ba43a9d344b.jpg

» Their comic attributes have made them useful figures for other forms of media as well, like radio shows and newspaper funnies.

– Don Quinn, creator and head writer of radio's hit sitcom *Fibber McGee and Molly* – when needing a worthy type of dog to mention on the airwaves – wryly chose the "Air Dale" 9 out of 10 times.

Like this, from the October 21st, 1941, show when the McGee's snooty neighbor Mrs. Uppington says she's unable to locate her French poodle 'Fifi' –

Oh, don't worry about her, Abigail. She probably eloped with some traveling Airedale.

Or this from June 3rd, 1941, when the young girl from across the street is talking to Fibber about her school play *Little Red Riding Hood,* where she has the role of the villain:

> *You – a wolf?*
>
> *Sure . . . I got a dandy costume too, mister. It's really an Airedale getup, but I look just like a wolf.*
>
> *Oh, Citizen Canine, eh?*

– Or, how about this tongue-in-cheek gem from the June 27th, 1916, edition of the *Chicago Day Book,* "Ain't Nature Wonderful!"

The Airedale

What is it, a doormat or a mop? Neither, Edna, this is Mitz, the aristocratic frouse.* The canine with the arctic nose and the whiskbroom coat of fur. The Airedale is a very dainty dog, light on his feet – like the usher at the ball park. When he gallops through the parlor, the piano is the only thing left standing.

Society people like the Airedale because it makes such a fool of itself. (There must be something in that old strip of chatter, "Birds of a feather flock . . . side by each.")

The under part of an Airedale's chin makes Niagara Falls look like the Sahara desert. The Airedale isn't particular what he eats. Anything suits him.

Airedales are very fond of children. Get one for the baby.

https://i.pinimg.com/564x/85/da/67/85da67c81
87e9169b6ef68e09e985c87.jpg

* Frouse is a slang combination of "friend" and "spouse."

— Airedale people will instantly relate to the drippy chin statement! It's a constant battle to dab them before our own personal terrier rex runs to the far corners of the house to shake themselves out like a spinning brush at the car wash.

THE 'LOST' WALKS WITH LEPORELLO ESSAY

When I came to write this book, in an effort to deal with my grief in the immediate aftermath of having lost him in 2011, I did so with a kernel of idea. That is because in 1999 I dashed off the original *Walks With Leporello* essay after a particularly engaging encounter with an Airedale admirer one morning. I placed the yellow pad upon which it was written in my 'work bin' to sleep, but I never forgot about the impetus that had led me to writing it. It was this that I revived twelve years later to write the current collection, and not the essay itself.

However, I'll provide it for the sake of its interest. I make no boast that what I wrote then is worthy for inclusion here, but it belongs nowhere else either.

Walks With Leporello 🍒   February 11, 1999

Sunny takes care of the dog in the mornings. And by 'take care of,' I mean takes him on his morning constitutional. The evening walk is mine. My responsibility for his post-meridian exercise consists of letting his pent-up energies – and probably his daily frustrations too – haul me or pull me up the hill to Buena Vista Park, chase his tennis ball around the darkly lit basketball court, and wag his tail when he looks back and up into my face. This is his health; his well-being manifested in body and spirit combined. I envy that ability, and as I walk, I feel a constant, regulating pressure to try and live as completely as he does; to be as settled as his contented eyes show me he is.

🍒   🍒   🍒   🍒

We meet all manner of people. He is a happy dog, and nine times out of ten, a person simply glancing at him – or more properly, their catching his eye on them – will send his tail swiping back and forth in a low and slow movement. His ears also sweep back and lie flat on his head in a way to humbly suggest "You recognize little ole me?" And he remembers people too, apparently knowing exactly who he's met before, for he evidently recalls their mannerisms, their attributes, as well as their looks, for all I know.

We encounter the same people on anything but a regular schedule. A year may go by and a person says something to us exactly the way someone once said it a year ago. I forget people, but not what they say. I'm sure Leppy forgets what sounds they may have uttered, but he remembers people, and has a call to treat them like long lost brothers and sisters.

One man, wearing army-surplus camo, came to a stop next to us as we were waiting to cross the street by a light one day and said matter-of-factly "These dogs were used to hunt lions in Africa. They're merciless after prey." And, as the suspicious man backed away, Leppy's ears went down, his tail began its tentative sweeping motion as he stepped towards the visitor. "Fearless," the camo man added as he stumbled away.

A second encounter with this same gentleman produced more of a conversation between us, and Leporello, sensing his chance, slid right between us, leaned on the fellow's legs. He also craned his head up to glance in the man's eyes. While still talking, the human's hand went down to stroke a very contented canine. Leppy's adorable cunning had worked its disarming magic yet again. When we encounter him these days, the man invariably starts the conversation by stating, and then asking, "Airedale. That's spelled E-I-R-E-A-D-A-L-E, right?"

He seems to think the breed has a connection to Ireland, and thus the Eire of his spelling.

Invariably, also, I reply – as if I'm back in one of those dreaded spelling bees of my fourth grade class – "A-I-R-E-D-A-L-E."

And his response every single time is, "Oh, A-I-R-E", with special emphasis on the E for some reason. Perhaps this is why he erroneously remembers the terrier name starts with one.

There's also a certain woman whom we've seen a few times with her boyfriend. They always seem to be approaching us from the front. The sidewalk in our block is not wide enough for three people and an Airedale to comfortably shoulder past one another. This requires that two of us – any two of us – halt and let the oncoming traffic flow by. But she's the one who always stops first. A smile comes over her face, her finger points knowingly. "That's the dog in the commercial, ain't it? The insurance commercial. That's him, isn't it?!" she proclaims with her voice excited and sounding just as it would had she made way for a movie star. The first time I said that he wasn't the "commercial dog," but by the second encounter, I decided to give a vaguer, open-ended 'maybe he is / maybe he isn't' answer. I do it because it makes her happy. She has a real celebrity pooch tale she can tell her friends. Leppy likes her a lot. The excitement in her voice raises his own love of life like sap in a spring bough.

A notable contrast is made by the time we spend with a rather older gentleman – his manner low-key; his pockets full of dog treats – who lives around the corner from us in a Victorian house on Beaver Street. Whenever we encounter him, he's reserved but warm. His conversation generally kicks off with an emphatic, admiring, "Oh, Airedales! They sure are fine dogs." The man always strokes Leporello's flat head, teasing the tawny locks between the dog's ears. "In World War One, they were fearless on the battlefield." He holds my eyes. "Did you know that? They ferried supplies and medicine through the battlefields to the trenches, and no sniper would intentionally hit one, so respected were they. Brave dogs; fearless."

Leppy wags his tail, sensing he's the topic of discussions, loving all the gentle attention.

ళ ళ ళ ళ

My dog appears to feel the tremendous respect of those who knew his ancestors as intrepid aids to hunters. And also with the others, like the older gentleman, who know that the dogs they remember from their youths are still around, and that the Airedale's admirable personal traits have not yet been bred out of them to suit a world insistent on vanilla-flavored homogeny. While for me personally, I come to acknowledge how all learning is only about being open to experiences, especially those experiences given to us in unexpected pleasures, ways and terms.

Leporello and I learn through and because of time, circumstance, and opportunity, for one is seemingly meaningless without the others creating the appropriate context in which to appreciate them as a whole. In our walks together, we encounter moments where body and spirit may combine in natural ease. And how wonderful is that?